I GOT THIS!
–GOD

Dotty,

You are so beautiful!

God's got you.

DB

I GOT THIS!
—GOD

A Journey of Grace
Deborah Bennett

XULON PRESS

Xulon Press
2301 Lucien Way #415
Maitland, FL 32751
407.339.4217
www.xulonpress.com

All scripture quotations, unless otherwise indicated, are taken from the Holy Bible, New International Version®, NIV®. Copyright ©1973, 1978, 1984, 2011 by Biblica, Inc.™ Used by permission of Zondervan. All rights reserved worldwide. www.zondervan.com The "NIV" and "New International Version" are trademarks registered in the United States Patent and Trademark Office by Biblica, Inc.™

Printed in the United States of America.

Due to the changing nature of online dynamics, websites, links, social media forums and references, no guarantee is made of the permanent reliability of these references.

Printed in the United States of America.

Manufactured in the United States of America.

Author's Coaching: www.sweetlifeusa.com.

ISBN-13: 978-1-54562-797-6

Dedication

I dedicate this book to my two beautiful daughters and their families. I love you with all of my heart. You have endured so much of this journey with me. I am so thankful for your grace and love.

To my four stepdaughters and their families. You have been a blessing and an integral part in this journey. I love you all.

To my closest friends, my sisters in Christ, who have encouraged and supported me along the way.

To my loved ones – my husband, my mom and dad, brother, and aunt, who are with our Heavenly Father.

To all of the many friends, who God has connected me with over the years; I appreciate each one of you and what you have brought to my life.

To my ten beautiful grandchildren who are my heart, I pray that this book will be a legacy for you, that you might be encouraged and gain something from my journey. I pray that you will have an understanding of how much God loves you, and that He wants to be with you, and that you will know His grace.

Acknowledgements

I acknowledge You, Heavenly Father, my Lord and Savior, Jesus Christ, for saving me from myself, for loving me when I didn't love myself, for believing in me, for being faithful, for teaching me and transforming me, for rescuing me, for grace and mercy when I didn't deserve it, for giving me life in abundance, for the blessing of family, friends and ministry, and for an extended family in your Kingdom!

Thank you to my sister-in-law for reading along with me as I wrote, and, for being my cheerleader and encouraging me.

Thank you to a dear friend – you know who you are, for reading along the journey with me and for sharing your wisdom.

I acknowledge my beautiful Author Coach, Jacqueline Arnold. I couldn't have written this book without you. I know it was a divine appointment the day I met you.

Thank you for teaching, encouraging, and, believing in me.

Table of Contents

Introduction

L ife can be really messy – sometimes because of the decisions we make, and,

sometimes, simply because we live in a fallen world.

I had 12 good years with a loving, functional family, and then, life as we knew it,

was turned upside down. It was the beginning of a life-long journey of loss, trials,

and tribulation, grief, and despair. Throughout my journey, God has given me the

ability and strength to pick up the pieces to survive and persevere. He has always provided for me and my family. There have been several turning points of surrendering, yet, even though I was leaning closer to God, I still was doing things that I shouldn't.

I learned how patient is our loving God. He has patiently waited on me to give up those things of this world that were separating me from knowing the fullness of Him. We will never be able to comprehend just how BIG our God is, but I am beginning to get a glimpse.

In this book I will share many poor choices I have made throughout my life and the things I have done.

As Paul said,

> *"But he said to me, "My grace is sufficient for you, for My power is made perfect in weakness. Therefore, I will boast all the more gladly about my weaknesses, so that Christ's power may rest on me. That is why, for Christ's sake, I delight in weaknesses, in insults, in hardships, in persecutions and, in difficulties. For when I am weak, then I am strong."*
> —2 Corinthians 12:9-10

As we journey together, I will share about loss and grief, about my transformation, restoration, victories, blessings, and, God's grace upon my life. My prayer for those who are reading this book is that you will begin to grasp the hope and love of Jesus Christ and understand that knowing Jesus is the only way to feel whole and complete and that He will meet all of your needs.

I hope that you will feel encouraged and begin to find purpose in your lives, to know that no one is perfect and that God chooses those who are lost and broken. Our time here on earth is short; God has us on a journey for Him and His purposes. It is not about us, but for us to love others, and to glorify God in this short span of time.

God has taught me to embrace the journey. He created us and knew us by name before we were even born. He knows our past, present, and future. He has been writing our story since the beginning of time. He is already in our tomorrows.

"For I know the plans I have for you,"
declares the LORD*, "plans to prosper*
you and not to harm you, plans to
give you hope and a future."
—Jeremiah 29:11

I will share how God called me to a ministry that could only come from Him and how He equipped me for this purpose.

> *"Now may the God of peace...equip you with everything good for doing His will, and may He work in us what is pleasing to Him, through Jesus Christ, to whom be glory forever and ever. Amen."*
>
> —Hebrews 13:20-21

He weaved everything from my past together for a better purpose for my future, and used it purposefully in my ministry. He took the grief and the sadness, the poor choices and the sin; He took the tears and the pain, and molded it into something beautiful. God makes beauty out of ashes.

> *"...to bestow on them a crown of beauty, instead of ashes, the oil of joy instead of mourning, and a garment of praise instead of a spirit of despair. They will be called oaks of*

righteousness, a planting of the Lord
for the display of His splendor."
 —Isaiah 61:3

I love the lyrics of this particular song by Michael W. Smith:

"Like a rose trampled on the ground,
You took the fall
And thought of me
Above all"

Michael W. Smith, *"Above All,"* recorded 2001, *Worship,* Reunion Records, Issued 2001.

Come along with me to see how God has revealed His grace throughout my life and has prepared me to use what I have walked through for the good of His Kingdom. May my journey bless you and give you hope in yours.

CHAPTER ONE

TRAGEDY AT TWELVE

It was a stormy evening, loud thunder and lightning created turmoil in the summer sky as I was preparing for bed that Tuesday evening, away at camp. It was the summer before my 7th grade school year and I had looked forward to sleeping away from home and all the summer fun in store for me. My friends and I were getting ready for bed in our cabin when a couple of ladies from my neighborhood unexpectedly came walking through the door.

I knew that something was up and I was immediately alarmed. The ladies told me to gather my things and they were there to take me home. I was confused; I was just preparing for bed and summer camp had barely just begun.

They didn't give me much of an explanation and I sensed from their demeanor that I wasn't to ask too many questions.

Once we were in the car, I was told that my eight-year-old brother had been in an accident. Something told me that he was dead, so I just asked them. They exchanged nervous glances to one another, and then back to me, again. They had wanted my parents to be able to give me the news, they were just sent to bring me home, but once I asked the unspoken question, they had to be truthful.

I was 12 years old and I could barely process what they were telling me. They kept it simple, just answering with a head nod or two. Hearing news like that didn't even make sense to me; of course it never does to someone in a crisis, having to process such an unfathomable thing. Life, as we knew it, had changed forever, and, I would never be the same.

Once I was home, I went running through the house to find my parents. There were already so many people – too many people, some who I did not know. I wondered why all these strangers were in my home. It was like a fog that I was trying to see my way through, just to find the people that I loved; I was so scared. I found my parents in their bedroom; they were both very emotional with so many tears streaming down their faces. It was really hard at such a young age to see my parents so upset like that, but to see my dad so broken was one of the hardest things I have ever encountered. It was a night I will never forget. We just held on to each other for a very long time.

My brother was four years younger than me. He was my only sibling. We had a happy childhood while he was alive. I don't remember too much about that time. It seems that we have a built in defense mechanism that represses memories around trauma. I'm sure I did this. My life with him is a blur; however, I do have some precious pictures that help me remember that life before he died.

My dad had taken my brother on a weekend trip just before I left for camp. Before they returned on Sunday, my mom took me off to camp, so I didn't see my brother for several days before that evening the neighbor ladies arrived. From what I was told, that Tuesday afternoon, my brother's best friend was with him playing in our neighborhood. As I mentioned, there was a rain storm that day. My brother and his friend were crossing the street to get to our house. My brother went first and darted out from behind a parked car; another car came down the hill, and without any notice of his approach, hit him. I understand he was dead shortly after arriving at the hospital.

I always remember my mom telling me that he said a couple of words, that his chest hurt, and he couldn't breathe well. Those were the last words she ever heard her baby boy say. It was so hard losing a sibling, but I cannot even fathom the pain and hurt my mom and dad experienced, and, God willing, hope to not ever experience.

His friend had to witness that horrific tragedy and is still affected by it to this day. My heart has always hurt for him. He had to go and tell my mom about the accident, then went to sit on a stoop to wait on his mother. That is some trauma for a 10 year old to have to witness. I am so sorry for you, my friend.

Those days around my brother's death are the last days I remember ever grieving with my parents about him. I remember being at the funeral home and seeing his casket, but I chose not to look in – it was a little too freaky for me. I just wanted to remember him as he was – that sweet and cute little boy that let my best friend & I dress him like a girl and who played with us or did whatever we wanted. He was such a good sport.

I remember going to the gravesite to bury my brother that day. On our way, I was looking back at all of the cars behind us – there were so many, you couldn't even see the end of the line. In a 12 year-old girl's mind, that was pretty impressive. There were so many who came out to support our family and loved on my parents during that time

Once we buried my brother, our life went back to what others may think of being normal. There was a day soon after his funeral that I came home from school and all that would have reminded me of my brother had been erased from our home. There were no more pictures, his bedroom had been changed to look like a guest room, and all of his belongings had been taken out. And, just like that, I was an only child; we never spoke about him again.

We never grieved together anymore; we just went on with life as though nothing had happened. I never understood it, and, until the most recent years, did I grasp that I can never judge how my parents coped because I had not walked in their shoes, grieving a child. I know for me, that the situation was very unhealthy. I didn't really deal with that grief until the most recent ten years of my life.

But, time passed, and, with the passing of time, my father passed also. I have to tell you about a dream I had after my father passed away. I was away on vacation with my family. The dream was so vivid this one particular night. I was dreaming that the phone rang and when I answered, my dad was on the line. He told me there was someone there that wanted to speak to me. He put my brother on the line and I heard a small voice say, "Hi, this is Sandy."

That's all there was to the dream and the phone conversation with my brother, Sandy, but let me tell you, it touched me deeply – what a gift from God it was. My dad was our connection. That dream has brought me a lot of peace over time.

I am not really sure, but I always suspected that it was mostly my mom that decided to do life the way we did. About 15 years ago or so, my mom called me and said that she had put a picture of my brother up on the wall. That was the first time since 1966 that he was acknowledged in my family. She said every time she walked down the hall, she would cry. That was huge for her to hang that picture, and I was so proud of her for finding the strength to do so.

We didn't talk about my brother much until the last few years of her life and for that I am sad, but I have accepted it. It is always such a blessing when I reconnect with someone who knew my family before that tragic day. They are able to help me with memories of my brother and reminisce what my family was like in those days.

In time, as we started living life again, I had the most amazing high school years. My parents were very supportive of me. They were always there to encourage me. They praised me often, maybe a little too much, but I was happy to take it. I loved high school and all my friends. I marched on the drill team and, at the time, decided I wanted to do that for the rest of my life – I loved it. My parents opened up our home to my friends and supported my constant activities. There were always kids in our house.

I have to mention that I was a pool shark and my dad loved to challenge his friends to try and beat me. It was just one of the ways we connected in fun.

I have always been so blessed to have an abundance of friends. Friends are really important to me. My mom loved to cook and was the best at cooking, so she always had great food for us, which was a real draw for friends to come over. She was the queen of hospitality. Mom also loved playing games with me and my friends. Our house was full of young people, and I know that made my mom happy. It must have helped to fill up her days, and, perhaps, ease some of her grief.

My dad was a really hard worker, too hard, in my opinion. He wasn't home much, but I loved being with him when he was. He was my best friend. He was such a fun dad. I worked for him in his business for several years and I loved it. We had such a special relationship, and for that I will always be grateful. He always took care of me and I just knew that he would 'rescue me' and be my security for the rest of my life, or so I thought. I look back on time, and believe his workaholic behavior was his way of coping with the grief. We really had a great time in my teenage years; I have so many fond memories.

Life was busy and full for me, both at school and outside. I was very active in my youth group at church. I was saved in my younger years, before my brother died. I don't remember much about it, I just know that I was. I do remember being immersed in baptism. I remember that very vividly. My brother and I shared great memories of vacation bible school together, too. I remember standing outside the church and as we all entered the church we were singing '*Onward Christian Soldiers.*' Isn't it funny, the things that stand out in our memory?

Even though life seemed to be full of fun in the years after my brother passed away, one of the things that was really hard for me was that because of his loss, I always felt over-protected by my parents. Most days, I just went along with it, accepting that they were trying so hard to not lose another child, but I am telling you, sometimes it was smothering. I tried so hard to never rock the boat for them. I felt like I became their protector in some ways. I became a people pleaser because of those circumstances and already was learning the behavior of being non-confrontational, which would not help me in the years going forward and the life events I would face.

All of these years, I have had a hard time with the fact that we didn't grieve my brother's death properly, or talk about him anymore. I felt so alone in that grief. After my father's death in 1997, I began to deal with the affects of all the years of the silence. A couple of years ago, I had to write a short autobiography for a Pastoral Education class I was taking. While I was reflecting and speaking of my brother's situation, God revealed a special gift my parents had given me. As I wrote how wonderful my high school years were, and how they were some of the best years of my life, I began to ponder how could I have just tragically lost a brother, and in the next breath, have such a great few years afterwards. I then, realized that my parents sacrificially put their pain and suffering aside to make sure that I was not affected. They gave me the best they could have in the years to come. It was their way of protecting me. I am so humbled that they could do that. They made life all about me, without showing the pain and agony they must have felt. They had to be dying on the inside, holding in their grief. Through their gift of love, they helped me to have the confidence I have today. They loved me like I was the only one on the planet. They were fun and generous. I learned so much from them.

I have been wowed by this gift and thank God for opening my eyes! I am so sorry for the pain mom and dad carried, and still, I am sorry that I couldn't have shared more of the pain with them, but humbled by the sacrifice they made for me. One day, we will all be together again and I will be able to thank them.

The loss of my brother was the first of many life changing events to bring me to where I am today. My parents sacrifice reminds me a little of Jesus' sacrifice for us. He suffered and took on so much pain so that we could live an abundant life.

God was already molding me from the beginning, He was showing me grace, and I didn't even know it.

CHAPTER TWO

DOWNWARD SPIRAL

With fall quickly approaching, my best friend and I were planning to head off to college for the adventure of our lifetime. My high school years were the best. It was exciting and sad at the same time to graduate. We had such a great class, I loved my classmates and none of us wanted to leave one another. On the other hand, I was excited because my friend and I had all these plans for our future and we would soon be living a new adventure.

She and I had already been accepted into the school that we wanted to attend and were planning to try out for drill team when we arrived. Both of us marched at our high schools and had big dreams of marching again while away at college. I had plans to be a math professor for a college; math was my favorite subject in school and I loved the challenges it gave me. I already knew that I enjoyed helping others learn. I was eager to get started in my new direction, with my new dreams, until...

I met a young man right, out of high school, and my plans quickly began to change. This guy was tall and lanky with dark hair, and had great dimples, with a cute smile, and, he swept me off my feet. Before I knew it, I had fallen for him.

Remember that I had accepted Jesus into my heart as a young child, and, I was heavily involved with the youth group at church, and the personal relationship I had with Jesus Christ was so important to me, that I wanted to live in His will always?

Well, my mind and heart quickly missed a beat and got swept away after meeting my man. I was praying to God for a sign that he would be the right one for me. One day he went to church with me, and during that service, he accepted Jesus into his heart. In my thinking, that was clearly a sign for me to marry him. I was missing something, and was certainly not thinking clearly. My future husband, who had just been baptized, introduced me to drinking and partying, and I got caught up in the frequent indulging with him. I was soon having sexual relations outside of marriage even though I knew better. I had known what God's word says about premarital sex.

> *"Marriage should be honored by all, and the marriage bed kept pure, for God will judge the adulterer and all the sexually immoral."*
> —Hebrews 13:4

It just goes to show how we can so easily justify what is right in our minds because of something we so desperately desire. I agreed to marry my husband in February of 1973 and traded my dreams for college. My best friend was not happy with me, which is probably an understatement. I was abandoning her and our dream together for drill team, college, and a bright future.

We had a big church wedding. In my 19-year-old heart, I was so happy. I was making a home, learning to cook, learning how to be a wife and keep up our home, and work full time. We were having a great time and feeling as if we were on top of the world. Six months went by and I felt like we were still on our honeymoon, until one night, my life, again, turned upside down.

My husband said he was going to see a friend and never came home. I was confused and worried sick. A friend of mine came to my apartment and stayed awake with me all night, comforting me the best she could. I was frantic; we called hospitals, police stations, and friends, but could not find him. The following morning about 10:00 a.m., he called me to say that he was not coming home and that I should consider packing up and going back to my parent's home.

Devastation is probably not a strong enough word to describe how I felt. I was traumatized; I just couldn't believe it. I thought we were still honeymooning and here he was ending our marriage. I have never before, or since that time, had such the temper that he brought out in me over his decision and how he managed it. I learned where he was that morning and drove over there, determined to get to the bottom of things. I walked in the door to find him sitting in a chair, eyes glazed over from drugs. I hauled off and slapped his face because I was so angry. After that morning, I was awakened to the fact that before me, he was heavily into drugs, and this was part of the cycle he was caught up in. He must have put them on hold when we started dating and I guess after some time, it was too much for him to not 'use' anymore. He needed to get back to his old life. That opened my eyes to the great big world, and to know that sometimes people are not what or who they seem. We can look for discernment in God's will for our lives and think we know what it is, but we need to make sure we are walking in His truth and following His ways before we jump in.

I moved out and into an apartment with a couple of girlfriends. They were very gracious to let me move into their space, and, as I was reminded recently by one of them who let me share her bed, I was not the easiest to room with. I am sure the anger welling up in me, and the grief stuffed way deep down, was impacting me.

To make matters worse, I was beginning to find my way into the alcohol and drugs scene to escape, too, and was keeping her up late when she had to leave early for work each day. Please accept my apology, my friend, after all of these years. God opens blind eyes.

I was grieved and became obsessed over my ex-husband. In my earlier high school years I was a good kid and never caused any trouble or did anything wrong. Now, I was choosing a path that was out of character for me. I was working a full time job and partying into the late hours, indulging in alcohol and drugs. I found myself being promiscuous with many men. I look back on that time and ask myself why, what was I looking for? I knew Jesus, but had more or less put Him on a shelf. When I was hurt so badly by my ex-husband, I did not lean on the Lord, I rebelled and chose a life of instant self-gratification. I was looking to fill the hole in my heart in all the wrong places. This behavior went on for several years. I had moved out on my own and into an apartment. It made it more convenient to come and go as I pleased and it gave me a space where I could invite whomever I wanted into my home. Don't you know that I made God sad with those choices, but you know what else I do know? He never stopped loving me, even though I was not communicating with Him, or following His ways. He loves us unconditionally, always remember that.

As life moved forward and I began to lean on Jesus (as you will read in later chapters), I was questioning why I would have chosen these past behaviors. I believe that I was weak and vulnerable from the loss of my brother and the dysfunction we had in our home. I told you that I was so happy in my teens when living at home but there was something missing and that was not being able to grieve my brother's death. I was burying my grief, and my sense of feeling lost in the drugs and alcohol, and mostly enjoying the relief and the instant gratification from the promiscuity. What are you running from and what are you using to fill the hole in your heart? If you are like I was, I hope you would reach for the loving arms of Jesus, instead.

I continued to see my ex-husband on and off, even after our separation. I just couldn't shake him. I would go to the places that he would typically be, just hoping to bump into him. Every time I was trying to get over him and move forward, he would knock on my door in the middle of the night. I would let him in and sleep with him. The next day I would be so upset with myself and then, I would do it all over again.

18

I was so sick of being treated like he was treating me that I made a decision to let go and was finally able to move on.

One night I was at a friend of my ex-husband's apartment. His friend's brother was there and I felt attracted to him. One of the things that I liked about this new guy was that he didn't do drugs and 'only' drank beer – go figure. I thought that was such an improvement from my ex-husband's style of partying, that I was attracted to him, thinking it would make it safe and better, and, that it was a very good choice on my part. I was beginning to understand that I didn't want to be around the drugs as much anymore, not as heavily, anyway – I didn't say I had stopped using drugs. God was convicting me, but I had been so slow to surrender to His convictions. Over the years, it has taken me longer to really know and hear God's calling or prompting upon my life. Some might say I am a little stubborn! But He is patient and persistent. He goes after the one – the prodigal son.

Do you hear that I was still moving from one guy to the next? I will say though, that when in an actual relationship, I have always been faithful to the one I am with. When in a committed relationship, I am loyal. I did, however, engage in several relationships with men who were separated from their wives, but not yet divorced. As a Christian, I know, that is not acceptable, but those were the choices I was making then.

In hindsight, I can see how God has always protected me, even when I was not asking Him. There were so many things that I did that could have prevented me from being here today, like riding around Interstate-285 smoking weed at a speed of at least 45 MPH. Only God could keep me from getting hurt and from getting stopped by the cops. To this day, I'm so utterly thankful, and amazed.

I had a friend who was dealing marijuana. I was pretty good at saving money, so I had a little put away. I decided that it would be a 'smart investment' to go in with him to purchase a supply. I went to my friend's home where he was keeping the supply that we had purchased and when I walked in the door, I was overwhelmed with how many large trash bags there were containing our investments.

I had not been in the house long when I looked out the large front window to see a police car parked in the driveway across the street.

Needless to say, I did not stay there long – I high-tailed it out of there! I now know that was God's grace that gave me that knowledge and instinct to run. The Holy Spirit was convicting me, even when I wasn't paying attention.

He has been showing me grace all along my journey, even when I couldn't see it at the time. I don't know why the consequences are different for each of us from the mistakes and choices we make that are not pleasing to God, but I do know that He has a plan that we don't understand and He works it all out in spite of our choices; for that, I'm simply grateful, and, especially, that He got me out of that situation that night.

I recently read somewhere that intelligence is not what is important for successful living, but our character. It takes some people longer to build character than others.

> *"Therefore, since we have been justified*
> *through faith, we have peace with God*
> *through our Lord Jesus Christ, through*
> *whom we have gained access by faith*
> *into this grace in which we now stand.*
> *And we boast in the hope of the glory of*
> *God. Not only so, but we also glory in*

our sufferings, because we know that suffering produces perseverance, perseverance, character; and character, hope. And hope does not put us to shame, because God's love has been poured out into our hearts through the Holy Spirit, who has been given to us."

—Romans 5:1-5

CHAPTER THREE

PLAYING GOD

I mentioned in the last chapter that I had met a guy I was really attracted to; he would eventually become my husband. He was a cute dark-headed guy with a charming personality. He was the life of the party and we really hit it off. We began to date and very quickly decided to live together. That is what we did back in the "hippie movement" days. It seemed that everything was acceptable – drugs, alcohol, sleeping around, sex outside marriage and 'shacking up' with one another. Not many of us thought much about it; it was the norm. It was fun and self-gratifying. I didn't have a care in the world. I did exactly what I wanted to do. I still had left God on the shelf so to speak and never gave a thought as to what He might think about what I was doing. I knew God was there, but had turned away from Him, not leaning on Him, but my own desires.

I ended up pregnant by the man I was going to marry. That unexpected pregnancy really threw me for a loop; it was so inconvenient. I had so many excuses not to have that child. I didn't want to go into the next marriage with a child because I had already been so hurt by my first husband and wanted to be certain that this guy would marry me because he loved me, not because there was a child in the picture. What a terrible excuse. It really was all about me.

I wasn't thinking of the child. I didn't really want children. I wanted to live life, follow my dreams and have my career. It was just a terrible inconvenience for me all around and yes, I was extremely self-centered. So, I chose to have an abortion. Today, I know how wrong it was to make that choice, but I had no remorse at the time. My soon to be husband, and a close friend, went with me to have the abortion. I was totally disconnected from the reality of the procedure in spite of being saved; I didn't have a need to rely on God.

It is crazier still that the father of the child – and, my best friend, offered their support and didn't challenge the decision. Looking back on it, that in itself was so crazy. We were all about being in the world, definitely not about the Kingdom of God. For years, I thought it was ok that I had gone through with the abortion. I had made peace with it in my heart and mind and certainly had justified my decision. Putting it behind me, I never thought too much about it after the actual abortion. For years, I was pro-choice. I felt like we as women had the right to choose whether to have our children or not. I was playing God. Who am I to have that right? I am not God; that decision is for God alone – the Creator of all life. I do not ever have that right, or want it.

In scripture, God tells me that my child was wonderfully and fearfully made by Him. It was me that had made the horrible choice to end the life that God had given. It didn't matter the circumstances as to how my baby got here, God already knew the child and had plans and a God ordained purpose for her or him.

I met a young lady recently that told me she was to be aborted, but her grandmother intervened; now she is grown and loves the Lord with all of her being. She is a beautiful witness for Him and has had a mighty impact on others to choose life. In knowing that story, I recognized that by ending the life of my child, by that act, I may have intervened in a plan that God had for my child to have an impact on others, and possibly prevented someone from knowing Jesus. Who am I to make such decisions?

> *"For you created my inmost being; you knit me together in my mother's womb. I praise you because I am fearfully and wonderfully made; your works are wonderful, I know that full well."*
>
> —Psalms 139: 13-14

You see, it has been in just recent years that I have really faced the decision I made to terminate my child's life on this earth. Through my daughter's experience of choosing to have a child as a single mom, God opened my eyes to just how horrific my choice was in His eyes. My daughter was very courageous to make a choice to bring a child into this world and to raise by herself. I am so inspired and in awe of her. I have had the honor to walk alongside her and witness her journey, and watch how God has moved in her and her child's life.

When my daughter was in delivery I had the honor to be there with her. After hours of labor, she had to have a C-Section. I was able to see my granddaughter pulled out of her tummy. My daughter had huge tears rushing down her face and I was so hurt for her, she was experiencing the pain and pressure from the surgery, and, maybe she was a little emotional for all that was happening, too.

While being concerned for her and asking the anesthesiologist to help her, I was seeing that precious child enter this world. Her child (my youngest granddaughter), was born, and I looked into my granddaughter's sweet eyes and saw for the first time, what could have been my child. I saw what I was missing. I never thought of my child as a person until meeting this grand-daughter. I love every one of my grandchildren and they all have a special place in my heart. This time was different, because in a moment I recognized that she represented what could have been with my child that I aborted.

This child could not have been if my daughter had not been courageous to choose to bring her daughter into this world. It was an emotional revelation. I was full of remorse and had to repent and ask for forgiveness from our loving Father. There was a short period of grief from the realization, 'oh my gosh, I had taken my own child's life. What mother does that?' to, 'I do know that our gracious God has forgiven me and continues to love me unconditionally'.

He continued to show me grace in my journey even then, before I had this moment of realization from my granddaughter's birth, and still I wasn't aware. As a matter of fact, He would eventually give me two beautiful daughters. That is grace – the grace of a loving Father! This is a great reminder that when we ask Jesus into our hearts there is nothing we can do to earn God's love and grace and there is nothing we can do to lose it.

I am humbled and thankful to say that I had asked Jesus Christ into my heart many years ago and accepted Him as my Lord and Savior. I know that I will be in eternity with Him in His Kingdom when I leave this earth. I am excited about that for so many reasons but one thing that I am truly excited about is that I will meet the child that I aborted and will be able to put my arms around him or her for the first time. I believe it is a boy, but I will have to wait to see! What a glorious day that will be.

> *"Though my father and mother forsake me, the Lord will receive me."*
> —Psalm 27:10

CHAPTER FOUR

NEW BEGINNINGS

I married my children's father in 1975, after living with him for several months. In the beginning it was wonderful. We were young and passionately in love. We had a lot of friends and loved to party. It was a way of life for us for several years. We worked during the day and joined friends at night to eat and drink. I loved being with my husband in the early years. We both loved to dance; we even took disco lessons for a period of time. He and I won a twisting contest!

When I married, I knew that my husband was a deer hunter and fisherman and figured out that I better learn to hunt and fish with him or I would never see him. That had my mom astonished; I was a city girl and never had shown interest in anything outdoors like that before. I actually came to enjoy being out in the woods or on the water with him. I wasn't a diehard though, I didn't want to touch anything that I caught or shot and I didn't want to bait my hook. Yes, I actually did shoot a deer and then I was done sitting in a stand with my feet frozen. I did that with him for six years and that was enough. I did have a deer on the wall for a while and I was quite proud of it. It was pretty comical looking back on my days of hunting. I would tie myself in a tree stand for fear that I would get excited and fall out. I have had enough of that adventure and choose not to ever hunt again.

In 1977, the 'first best thing' in my life happened. I had my oldest daughter, and what a blessing she ended up being. I aborted my first child, and, in spite of this, I still didn't want children. I did not want to be inconvenienced with someone else to take care of. I wanted to continue to do what I wanted to do – selfishly. Apparently, God had other plans because I unexpectedly got pregnant and I am so grateful to Him today for that gift of life and second chances.

Once I found out I was pregnant, and of course was already married, it was a given, as far as I was concerned, that I was to have this child. I can't imagine my life without my daughter. God already had plans for her life as she is now grown with a beautiful, Godly family – her husband, a son and daughter. She is a wonderful mom and has been serving the Lord since she was a teenager. She has chosen to be obedient to her calling from God in ministry early in life, unlike me. She has been inspiring and encouraging young people all over the world in her ministry. What if I had not had her, who would have missed out on learning about Jesus? God has used her as a vessel to touch many lives over the years. I am always learning and inspired by her.

In 1980, the 'second most important day' of my life happened. I gave birth to my second child, another beautiful daughter, and what strength she had right out of the womb! She is my strong-willed child. As an adult, she has been my rock, and has always stood by me. If you have a child that is tied to your hip, don't fret, that child is going to be the one to take care of you as you grow older. She has always been there for me in a moment's notice. I don't know if any of you have ever raised a strong-willed child (more about this in another chapter to come), but it can be a love/

hate relationship. I have adored her from birth, but she has challenged me. We have had many fights when she was a child. If I said it was black, she said it was white. She was always testing me and always disagreeing with me. God restored our relationship through grace. We can have fun with it now and have a beautiful relationship. God has used those challenging days to mold her into the person she is today. She is so helpful to me and others. She was learning to be so strong and independent. My daughter is a hard worker and brilliant. God has been doing something wonderful in her life. I love watching Him mold her into what He has planned for her. My daughter is a beautiful young lady and a wonderful mom and has blessed me beyond measure.

Both of my girls have raised their children to know Jesus and grow them in their faith since birth. I couldn't ask for anything more. I did not get them into a church until they were a little older. It makes my heart smile to see the love my girls and their children have for our Lord and Savior.

One day, while registering my oldest daughter for preschool, God sent an angel who would become my best friend for the next 38 years of raising our children together, parenting, and just doing life. She has been my support, my confidant, and my sister in Christ. She knows what I need without even asking. She loves my kids and grandchildren. She has been all and more than I could ever ask in a friend. She has been there for me through every crisis in which I have walked through, with the exception of the loss of my brother. She knows my joys and sorrows. You will hear more about how God has used her to love on me in my journey in pages to come. I'm eternally grateful for you, my friend. God gives us people in our lives to be our hands and feet. I am forever grateful He sent me such a dear friend to walk alongside me.

Let's get back to my marriage – we were learning how to be parents and loved our girls so much. I loved being a mom. I was a room mom for many years and loved my children's friends and classmates. I loved supporting the girls through the years in their extracurricular activities, sports, and, so forth. Many nights my husband and I would hang out with our friends and their families. There was a lot of drinking and partying going on though. As years went by I began to realize just how much our lives revolved around alcohol. I was at fault just as much as my husband. It was a priority for us. We made sure that whatever we did at night, on the weekends, and when we traveled, involved alcohol. We took trips without our children often, more than we should have. My mom, dad, and aunt lived close by and were always willing to keep the children. I am not sure that was a blessing or a curse. It might have just been an enabling act to allow us to continue down the path we were on. I am thankful for all of them though, especially in later years when I was a single mom. Most of the trips that were taken with my children were with my mom and me. My husband and I were too focused on ourselves when going away. We were living in sin and having a blast. Our priorities were all messed up.

My husband worked with my father in a business they owned and they did very well financially. They were making a lot of money and bringing home cash for my mom and me to spend. There really wasn't anything that we lacked. We could buy pretty much whatever we wanted.

My husband and I bought a houseboat in 1984 and kept it for a couple of years. We had a blast at the lake. My girls loved being there and making new friends. Once again, we were partying hard. Today, I look back on those years and recognize God's grace all over us. There were so many ways someone could have been hurt with all the craziness going on around the water.

There was one incident where my oldest daughter, who was about five years old at the time, fell off a ladder and fractured her wrist. My husband was off fishing at the time. Once he returned and learned what had happened, he cursed her out for doing that, screaming and yelling at her. I was appalled and so hurt for her. He had no compassion for her.

This is the type of behavior we would witness over and over and it wasn't fun. I did the best I could with what I had and who I was. I was the protective parent because my husband, as I had begun to understand, was an alcoholic. There was no stopping him. After that incident, I began to see the difference. I would have a few drinks and be done. He, on the other hand, didn't have a grasp on time or how much he was drinking, or when to stop.

I was finally growing up and the alcohol was becoming less important to me. I never said I stopped having a drink or two. The difference between the two of us was that he could not stop once he started. There was a lot of verbal and emotional abuse while he was drinking. My girls and I became frightened by him. He intimidated us. He would call my children and I names, always putting us down. He would fly off the handle and scream. We walked on egg shells, never knowing when he would blow up.

Years later, as I looked back on our lives, it made me very sad that I couldn't protect my children from the pain that he caused us. I was always afraid to rock the boat for fear that if I stood up to him someone would be hurt. As a mom, that was a terrible feeling to not be able to protect my family; I felt so helpless!

Back in 1981, my husband was coming home from work and getting really drunk early in the evening, to the point that he was nearly comatose and would just sit in his chair all evening. I was so concerned for him; I thought he was really depressed over something. I would question him, but no answers. This went on for months. I didn't know what to do, I was doing the best I could to take care of my children and prevent him from having a negative effect on them from him. Well, there was no way I could keep them from seeing his behavior.

There was one evening that the phone rang, he answered it, and after a brief conversation which I couldn't hear, he suddenly handed the phone to me. Well, there was a woman on the other end of the call, and that night I learned she had been having an affair with my husband for about a year.

I felt like a knife had just pierced my heart and, after this brief, life-changing phone call, I was in a state of shock and anger, and had feelings of betrayal seething within me. All the trust I had for him had just left me.

Wow...what to do now? I thought, after hanging up the phone.

The children were in another room. They were so young. I hung up the phone and asked him if it was true and he admitted that yes, it was. That explained why he had been so much more inebriated than usual for so long, because he could not live with himself over it, so he explained to me.

We had a really good talk; he explained it all to me. The affair was with someone whom he worked with. He said it was over. He asked me to forgive him. She had been saying she would tell me if he didn't give up his family, funny thing is that she also had a family. When she called, she was threatening to blackmail him again and he was done with her and decided to take a chance to let me know about it.

What was even worse – if there could be anything worse, is that he was seeing her while I was pregnant. My heart was so broken. I have done a lot of things that are not morally correct but I have never been unfaithful in a relationship. It was so hard for me to comprehend. I was traumatized and overwhelmed, and left with an aching heart.

We decided to talk it out, put it behind us, and try again. It was hard, but I was so willing because I believed in us. I loved him and I wanted it to work. I knew that I had to do my part and not keep bringing it up and he had to work to earn my trust again. We moved on with our life and decided to build our dream home for a fresh start. It seemed that when we were involved in projects, we were much happier; putting our focus on other things, and keeping busy made it easier to keep moving on.

We had fun driving to log cabins to look at different styles, which is what we wanted to build and we were elated to have our dream home, too. Our children were excited about living in the country and filled with anticipation about the process. We ended up building a large, custom built log home; we thought we had died and gone to heaven. This was our new focus, so many projects to keep us busy. He was still drinking and abusive in his language to us, but we had something that we thought was going to make us happy and create positive change in our family. I was hanging on to hope that all that we had and were creating would change the way things were.

One afternoon we were working outside in the yard when I received a call from our builder. Well, he accidentally spilled the beans in something he said and I realized there were people coming to our house for a surprise house-warming party. I ran out and told my husband to get in and shower, that people were coming. Oh my gosh, it was so much fun! All of a sudden, a lot of cars were driving up our long driveway honking horns to surprise us. We had to act surprised but we really were, anyway.

There was so much love that came in each one of those cars. Our friends and family came with all the food and drinks to celebrate our new home. We were blown away.

Life was all mixed up. We had some really fun times as a family, with my husband and children, but then in the next breath it was challenging and confusing and hard. My children and I were good when he was away at work or hunting or fishing. Once he walked in the door, we never knew what to expect, was he going to be in a good mood or would he be abusive? How were we supposed to act around him? Maybe if we put on our best behavior, he would be nice. What could we do for him to make him happy?

My oldest daughter began to have migraine headaches every day after school as soon as she got home. We learned later it was related to her anticipation of how daddy was going to be when he came home. He would come home and expect everyone to greet him at the door and would be mad if the children did not. I tried to tell him that he was the parent and should go to them. Once my husband moved out of our house, she never had those headaches again; it is amazing how stress can affect our health.

Somewhere in the late 80's, I began to see that our lives were truly falling apart and that I needed something more than all that we had. From the outside, it looked like we had this perfect little family with two beautiful girls, a hard working daddy, a stay at home mom, a beautiful big home and lots of big toys.

Remember when I said that I had put God on a shelf? One day when my children were in school and my husband was at work, I stood in the kitchen of my big house with all the things that I thought could make us happy, but I realized how truly miserable I was. There was the realization that I needed to take God off of that shelf and lean on Him. I had so many reasons to stop running away from Him and into Him.

Our lives were crumbling from the pain and suffering of the abuse in the house. There was so much stress and I no longer knew where to turn. I was depleted and had no confidence in myself anymore. My children and I had suffered enough of the ridicule, the rages of anger and walking on egg shells, not ever knowing how we were going to be treated.

I am so blessed to have had the foundation of Jesus from the time I was saved as a little girl. I am going to say it was the Holy Spirit that was nudging me that particular day. I was in a very vulnerable place and knew we needed God more than ever. God had always been there for me, but I had turned my back on Him time and time again.

I had placed all of my hope and dreams in my husband, our family, and the things that we had. In the midst of all that was happening, I recognized that I was this emotionally needy person who was clinging on to my husband for dear life, and I was smothering him. He used to tell me this exactly, but I didn't get it because I was all caught up in his actions and judging him.

From those years, I learned God is the only one that fills our emptiness, not anyone or anything other than Him. I am not sure that turning my back on God was intentional, but, life and the enemy got a hold of me and I was spinning out of control.

Our God is so patient. I was like the prodigal child that wanted to return to Him.

> *"The son said to him, 'Father, I have sinned against heaven and against*

43

you. I am no longer worthy to be called your son."

"But we had to celebrate and be glad, because this brother of yours was dead and is alive again; he was lost and is found."
—Luke 15: 21, 32

It was a life-altering day and from that day forward I began to change. I began to seek help from others, and I started with Al-anon. I had learned about Al-anon (a support group for friends and families of alcoholics), from a friend. It was life-changing when I started going. I was going to three meetings a week for several years. There, I began to learn how to stop enabling my husband in his addictions. He needed to be able to realize the consequences of his actions and behaviors. I was learning how to set boundaries and how to be assertive in truth and love.

I started coming home at night and sitting with my children to teach them what I was learning. I was teaching them to love their daddy and hate the alcohol, and how to separate the two. We were to have compassion for him, but did not have to tolerate the behavior. For the first time in many years, I understood that my children and I were people and not door mats – someone that could be run over and trampled on. I was beginning to understand how much God loved my girls and me and that He didn't want us to be hurt by my husband. God grieves when we suffer. I learned also that my husband was hurting. He had a disease that he had not admitted to but it was hurting him. I still loved him and continued to want him to get help and healthy.

One day, a locksmith came to my house and once he completed the job I hired him for, we had a conversation about Jesus out in the driveway. I knew of this guy but didn't really know him. I knew that he attended a church. I was telling him a little of my story and how I really wanted to get back into the church but was hesitant because I wanted my husband to go with us and that he was not interested.

The locksmith suggested that I go without him, he said that it was my journey with God and perhaps my husband would eventually join us because of my influence. (I am sorry to say that never happened). The locksmith will never know how profound that statement was for me.

The girls and I started going to church and I was so glad to be there.

I was leaning on God and getting into scripture. I was reading all kinds of self-help books to include those on codependency. I was learning how I had begun to be codependent starting from childhood. I had experienced trauma that caused us to be a dysfunctional family and that is where my emotional neediness and codependency began. Life is such a process of learning about ourselves and allowing God to transform us to the person He created us to be. We make mistakes; we grow and make more mistakes. God is patient with us and uses all that we come through for the good of others and for His glory once we begin to surrender our lives to Him.

By this time there had been three more affairs of which I was aware. I was so desperate! Now that I was leaning on God more, I was so troubled considering a divorce. After all we had gone through, I still believed in my husband. I knew that the alcoholic disease caused him to do things that he might not ordinarily do. I wanted him to want to get well but that wasn't happening.

Our lives were spiraling downwards. He had left the business that he was in with my dad. He was not working anymore. He was very depressed and sometimes claimed to be suicidal. I was scared; I felt lonely in the situation. I had some amazing friends to talk to and share with, but I just didn't know what to do. I had not worked outside the home in many years so I had no idea how I would provide for my children.

One night, I had to get out of my house and just think. I drove to a pond nearby to go for a walk to ponder what to do next. I was looking for answers and there it was. My pastor was out walking also. He knew of my situation and we walked and talked. I told him my concerns about the vows I had taken when I married my husband and had already been through one divorce. He told me that God didn't want us to be treated like we had and that is was ok to leave him.

Do you know what kind of relief that was? This might not be the right answer for you, but I felt like it was a tap on the shoulders from God and that it was time to make some decisions. I still had the financial piece to think about and plan for, among many other things, but I was at a place where I would have rather been out on the streets with my girls than stay in that situation.

Today, I am so proud of my girls, they have done remarkably well and grown into beautiful girls and moms and have done so much better than I did at that age. They went through a lot and have risen above it all with God's help. His grace is nothing short of amazing!

CHAPTER FIVE

TIDAL WAVES KEEP COMING

All our hopes and dreams for our family were crashing down before us and then here comes my dad with more news that would change the course of our lives forever. My parents were a huge support system for all of us. Even in the midst of the storms with my marriage, I loved when they would spend time with our family, and that happened often. My girls loved being with them and spent many a night at their home.

Mom and dad loved us so much and were always there for us. My dad came to announce that after 41 years of marriage, they were getting a divorce. To tell you the truth, I think I was really numb to that news. I probably wasn't all that surprised. I had gone through so much pain and suffering that honestly, I don't even think I felt anything at the time. How much more God, can we withstand?

Not only was our family impacted by the divorce, but many other families and couples were affected, too. There were so many friends with whom my parents were close and hearts were broken. I had a great relationship with all of them. Many took sides with my mom, and my dad was devastated. They had done life together for years. I never condoned the actions of my dad, nor pointed to him as the cause of their break up, but always loved him unconditionally. He had done the same for me over the years regardless of what I did to hurt them. I am thankful for the few friends who stayed in touch with my dad and was gracious to him.

Years later I began to understand that life was probably not good between my parents for all of the years after my brother passed away. I can't imagine the pain they endured, and pray to God I never have to face anything similar. I do understand that family members grieve differently and sometimes couples fall apart after losing a child.

Those who knew my parents as their friends never saw anything but a fun loving couple.

Mom and dad loved to host a good party, loved to travel with friends, play bridge, golf, and so many other fun activities. They were amazing parents and grandparents. Knowing them, you would never know they were hurting. I believe on the inside, they suffered greatly. I am sorry that I never got to have those conversations with them, but I know they now rest peacefully and are with our loving GOD, and my brother.

I tell you all this because as their friends began to be ugly toward my dad, I became very angry. I loved my dad – no matter what, and, I hurt for him. It would be years later before I could forgive all of them. After my dad died, any-time I would see their friends, they were always so kind to me, but I needed them to understand that my dad **died**. I would silently be steaming, *you used to love him.* I needed them to tell me how sorry they were that he had passed away, and I didn't hear those words, except from a few. I would carry this bitterness and resentment for years, as it was painful to me.

My husband had decided to look for work again, and was offered an opportunity with a company in Alabama. He asked me to go there with him to look at the area to see if we wanted to relocate. Apprehensively, I went with him and saw such a difference in the area versus where we were coming from. I had to consider the children. Our marriage was in such despair that I made the decision not to join him. He decided to commute every week.

This was the beginning of the end for us, and maybe a divine intervention by God. The more he was gone, the better life was for the girls and me at home. Eventually, he would not come home for several weeks at a time. We were realizing that there was so much less stress in the house. There was peace for once and we were liking it. At one time my children agreed, and were thankful, as was I, to not be living every day with my husband in our home, due to the stress it brought; however they did miss him and the life they would dream to have with him. We could breathe for the first time. While he was away, I was able to begin to regain my strength with God's help, and pray for what was ahead, for guidance and discernment as to how to move forward.

I had learned that my husband was now living with a woman whom he worked with. He was only coming home about once a month. The last time he was home, was on a Sunday, the girls and I were getting ready to go to church. I asked him to make a decision that day to either give up his alcohol or his family. I told him that I no longer would choose to tolerate the behavior around his alcohol usage.

The girls and I left him in the house as we headed to church without him. When we arrived home there was a letter from him addressed to the girls saying he was sorry, but he had to go and would not return. That was a heart-wrenching emotional day! The girls sat with me on the sofa and cried for what seemed an eternity. Their dad had not chosen them and that was such a deep stab in the heart. I knew that life was going to get better, but my children's hearts were crushed that day. For awhile, I was so angry with him to make such a choice, but knew God was going to see us through in spite of his selfish decision.

My husband and I began divorce proceedings. It didn't take long. Fortunately, he agreed to what I asked for. We filed and it was done. It was a long time in the making. There is a grief around divorce. It is the loss and death of a relationship, a family, what you dreamed it would be.

It is hard for all of the family and others that are part of our lives, as well. Just as grief of a death, in separation and divorce, all family members respond differently.

Forgiveness is a choice and I had chosen to forgive my husband for all that we had come through. Had I not made that choice, there would have been such bitterness in my heart and it would have only hurt me. I also recognized later that I needed to forgive myself because of my participation. I am so thankful for God's forgiveness.

> *"But if you do not forgive others their sins, your Father will not forgive your sins."*
>
> —Matthew 6:15

I want to share a story about a young girl that became a part of our life. When I first met my husband I learned he had a 5-year-old daughter. She was beautiful and so sweet. He brought her to our apartment the first time I met her and left her with me to go hunting. *Whoa*, I thought to myself, *what do I do with this sweet little girl?*

If you remember, I didn't really have an endearment for children, so I didn't have any idea what we would do for the weekend. We visited her uncle who lived in the same complex, and I just spent time with her. I became fond of her; she was so easy to be with. Our days were numbered with her because her mom's new husband ended up adopting her and we were not allowed to see my husband's daughter any more after that for nine years.

Then there was a day when my husband received a phone call from my stepdaughter's mom to say that she had gone through a divorce and wanted to know if my husband wanted to see her again. She was 14 now, and, of course he said yes. He visited her first, before we told our girls that they had a half-sister and introduced them to her. The girls all got along so well and acted as though they had been together all of their years. That was a huge blessing!

In the beginning, I probably had the hardest time. The first time I met her mom, we were like two cats circling each other. I was making sure she was not a threat, of course, and was trying to figure out how to adapt to the new dynamics of our family. After some time, my stepdaughter's mom and I became good friends. She was such an inspiration to me. She was gracious and thankful for us being a part of her daughter's life. I was so young in my spiritual walk with the Lord and she was so much ahead of me, that I learned much from her; this was a hidden blessing.

This sweet surprise friend had many health complications including being legally blind because of diabetes. She never complained, and, loved Jesus. I watched how she endured the difficult challenges she had in life and was totally encouraged and in awe of her faith. She had been raising her daughter to know that faith and the love of Jesus.

Today, my stepdaughter is a beautiful daughter of God, a wife, an ordained pastor, and raising a family of three children to know God's love, just as her mother taught her. My stepdaughter has also learned from her mom courage and how to endure and persevere as she faces life's challenges – as she has had many. Her mom, I know, is so proud of what her baby girl has become today.

Because of her disease, my stepdaughter's mom always knew that she would not live a long life. When she received the news of my divorce, she was deeply concerned. She shared with me that she was so thankful to have me in her daughter's life and didn't think she would be around for many more years. She said she was secure in knowing I would be there for her. I assured her that my stepdaughter would always be a part of my family, regardless what the future held for my husband and I. I will say to this day, my stepdaughter and her family continue to bless me more than they will ever know.

We lost my dear, sweet friend when my stepdaughter was pregnant with her first child. I will forever be grateful for such a sweet friendship and having the honor to encourage and love her daughter and family. This is another time of God's amazing grace as He has shown me how to love all of my children and grandchildren. God can do amazing things as He transforms us. He has changed me and given me a heart to love all of my kids and grandchildren. I didn't think I ever wanted children, but He had a different plan, and, has given me so many more to love. I will tell of more of each of them in the chapters to come.

The grief over my broken marriage would have to go on a shelf, as it was time to get practical about life. Now, I needed to find a job for myself. Other than working as a Realtor for a couple of years while my children were really young, I had not done anything else for so long and didn't have any idea what I would do. A friend of mine who owned a mortgage company offered an opportunity to be a mortgage loan office at her company. I did really enjoy being in the real estate industry but didn't want to be a Realtor again, even though I had kept up my license. I decided to step out in faith and try the mortgage business. I did love math in school (Recall, I was actually planning to be a math professor had I gone on to college).

In January of 1991, I started at the mortgage company and learning the business. I had to wait 90 days to receive benefits and I was 100% commission from the start. It wasn't an easy beginning, but I was motivated to get that first closing and then more, being commissioned was a big motivator – if you don't close a sale, you don't have income.

I have always had an entrepreneurial spirit. I was blessed with that from my dad; he was the same. Well, in March of that year, something happened to my back and down I went. I was driving to work and crying all the way. I could hardly get out of my car. Finally, my friend prompted me to "go home and take care of yourself."

I did do just that and ended up in the bed for eight long weeks. I was not able to sit, stand or walk. Wow, what was God doing with me? Now I couldn't go to work, so I couldn't get paid and still, I had no insurance, so there I laid and waited. I was able to make calls from my bed and had papers all over the bed while I tried to work, but it wasn't the same.

My girls had gone through enough. Now, I couldn't even take care of their needs. God was about to show me so much during this time. That is where I really learned to pray and the power of prayer. I had a new Realtor friend that ended up with the same back pain and was down in her bed. I became her prayer warrior. God was teaching me how to minister, pray, and encourage others. She was probably the first person I had ministered to, now that I think of it. God is truly amazing as to how He works. He might have allowed all of these things to happen to us but I believe He was molding and trans-forming me to glorify Him in the process, and what a process it has been.

I was not able to get up from the bed to eat so I would raise up on my shoulder to have my meals. It is so hard to believe now that I ever went through that but if I get a twinge in my back, I say God please don't let me go to that place again.

I learned so much about the importance of community and caring for others. I had recently started back to church at the right time, because of that, there was a circle of women that would bring food to my house for the girls and I. One of the ladies that came to deliver the food ended up being someone I went to school with and we reunited and are great friends now. You just never know how and who God is going to connect you with. He is always orchestrating our lives for a purpose. My very best friend and angel was so faithful to me, and there to get my girls on the bus, make sure they were taken care of, drive me to the doctor in the back of her SUV so I could lay down and so on, she was always at my beckon call.

Another one of my beautiful sisters in Christ, with a great servant's heart, came to shave my legs...now that is a true friend. Goodness, there was a forest growing on them. My mom, dad, and aunt would each come to cook, feed me and the girls, and take care of us. We take so much for granted when we cannot move. I am forever indebted to all of those who served us through that time of need.

I mentioned earlier that I was part of an Al-anon group. The ladies brought the meeting to my bedroom since I couldn't go there. God can make all things happen and He saw that was a need for me, so He provided. We have to recognize the small things. We think He isn't paying attention but He is such a big God and knows just what we need when we need it.

> *"For I know the plans I have for you,"*
> *declares the* Lord, *"plans to prosper*
> *you and not to harm you, plans to*
> *give you hope and a future."*
> —Jeremiah 29:11

I was so scared some days, I was in so much pain and really wondered if I would ever get up. I was able to go to a doctor twice for a shot. Since I had no insurance and no income, other than child support, I had to wait it out. I was waiting on God. Someone gave me the book "The God I Love" by Joni Eareckson Tada. It is her story about her diving accident and becoming a quadriplegic as a young woman. I will tell you that God placed that book in my hands to understand that what I was going through was not about me but how I could glorify Him in the midst of my pain.

Her story is beautiful. I was already learning about my journey of grace through her and didn't realize it at the time. I did recognize, though, that I really didn't have any problems in comparison to her. I knew one day I would get up again and be able to move and she wouldn't, and what grace she portrayed through her life story! We can always find someone worse off than us and that is what God was showing me, that I had nothing to complain about and everything which to be thankful.

> *"We are hard pressed on every side, but not crushed; perplexed, but not in despair; persecuted, but not abandoned; struck down, but not destroyed. We always carry around in our body the death of Jesus, so that the life of Jesus may also be revealed in our body."*
>
> —2 Corinthians 4:8-10

CHAPTER SIX

WHAT ON EARTH WAS
I THINKING?

After my husband and I had divorced, life was different. It was a time of so many mixed emotions. I was so thankful to not have the stress and abuse in our home, but it definitely was a time of grief over the loss of a relationship after 15 years of marriage. It was the grief of what might have been and what I had dreamed of for my marriage and my family.

It was grief for my children not growing up with a loving father. It was grief over all of the benefits of being married and having a companion to share life with. I didn't quite know how to survive without a man in my life, even though it had been an unhealthy relationship. I had grown very needy over the years and constantly wanted someone in my life to depend on, to love on, and to make me feel better about myself.

I had been looking in the wrong places for fulfillment for years since my first marriage. Once, my husband had told me that I was smothering him. I really didn't understand that comment. At the time, all my focus was on him and what he was doing or not doing in our marriage. The worse our marriage got, and the more he pulled away from me, the more I clung to him. I was desperate, scared, had little confidence, and was becoming very unhealthy emotionally.

Once he was gone, I was free and on the prowl. I had begun to turn my life back to Jesus, but I still didn't get it. I had one foot in the Kingdom and one foot here on this earth living out my sinful nature. I acted out in many ways of which I am not proud. The night it hit me at my core was when my oldest daughter had had enough of my behavior.

"You are a whore!" my 14-year-old daughter said to me. What an eye opener that was for me to hear.

> *"If we claim to have fellowship with him yet walk in the darkness, we lie and do not live by the truth."*
> —1 John 1:6

A friend of mine and I had gone to a bar one Friday night. She and I met up with two guys we had never seen before. We were having a blast and decided to take off to the lake with them the next day. From that date to just a few days later, I invited this guy to move in with me. I was excited, because he was paying attention to me and wanted to meet my needs physically and emotionally. He was willing to be my companion and do life together.

He attended my younger daughter's softball games with me, (something her father never did for her). He was playing a part in a relationship I had starved for. He didn't know Jesus and I was not being obedient to the Word of God, – a very bad combination. My oldest daughter called me out on it after a couple of months of him being with us in our home. It was like I had gone into a world of my own and gotten lost. I was only thinking of myself, looking for that self-gratifica-tion, and it was so wrong of me. I was showing my children a poor example of what someone who loves Jesus looks like.

What was I thinking? I have asked forgiveness from my girls over the years for my actions. There are many days that those two months come rushing back to me. The remorse has been overwhelming for putting them through that craziness. I know they forgive me, and Jesus certainly does. Thank God for His amazing grace!

I had asked the guy living with us to move out and told him I didn't want to see him anymore. I am thankful that God used my daughter to say those words to me, however hard they were to hear.

> *"If we confess our sins, he is faithful and just and will forgive us our sins and purify us from all unrighteousness."*
> —1 John 1:9

God has had so much patience waiting on me to open my eyes to the truth. I still didn't get it. After that event, it became important to me to keep anything I was doing with men from my girls, but, what about from God? I just kept on putting my needs in relationships with men rather than Christ. God knows everything and we cannot hide from Him. I wasn't ready to surrender all to him. We have a choice in everything we do, either to listen to and satisfy our flesh or be obedient and glorify God. It is a conscious choice.

I really began to realize that I had an addiction to sex. I would crave that physical satisfaction and could not get enough. I was lonely, hurting, and hungry for love, no matter the source. What was happening to me? As Paul had said in the scriptures:

> "*I do not understand what I do. For what I want to do I do not do, but what I hate I do. And if I do what I do not want to do, I agree that the law is good. As it is, it is no longer I myself who do it, but it is sin living in me. For I know that good itself does not dwell in me, that is, in my sinful nature. For I have the desire to do what is good, but, I cannot carry it out. For I do not do the good I want to do, but the evil I do not want to*

do—this I keep on doing. Now if I do what I do not want to do, it is no longer I who do it, but it is sin living in me that does it."

—Romans 7:15-20

I had mentioned that I was attending Al-anon, again a support group for those who have loved ones or friends with a drinking problem. Al-anon or support groups are not the place for building relationships with the opposite sex.

However, there was a gentleman in the group that I was most attracted to for many reasons; he was kind, nice looking, had a gentle spirit, and knew Christ, and we had daughters that were in school together. I loved to dance and he was a wonderful dancer. We began to see each other and it was amazing. There was so much romance and passion between us. I had never been treated like he treated me, he was a gentleman. I discovered so many qualities in him that I wanted in a man that seemed like they would fit in a healthy relationship. There was one problem, we were both unhealthy from alcoholic marriages and two unhealthy people do not make a healthy relationship. I was trying to rescue him and that is a huge no-no. That is what caretakers do. We become caretakers from a dysfunctional relationship. We were in and out of the relationship, but I just knew I was falling in love with him.

While I was continuing to make poor choices, living a dysfunctional, unhealthy and needy life, there was still a journey of grace that I didn't recognize. God would show me later how He has used all of the choices I have made to work for the good of others. God has allowed me to make the same mistakes over and over again to come to a place of surrender. He has been orchestrating my life to become a testimony for Him.

CHAPTER SEVEN

MOVING FORWARD

Finally, the house sold after a very long seventeen months. Once my husband and I divorced, selling the home became my responsibility. It took forever and I was feeling quite discouraged. It was really hard for me financially to maintain along with taking care of the girls and working. While so much of our stress was gone and we were in some ways happier, it was an adjustment for all of us. The girls certainly had their perspective and each responded differently to the situation. Now it was time to find a new home and begin a new chapter of our lives.

My girls were away one weekend with their dad, and I went house shopping. I was trying really hard to find a home that would keep both of my girls in the same school district, but with my budget it was not happening. As I was driving around, I pulled into a neighborhood, turned a corner and there it was. It was in the spring and the yard was full of beautiful azaleas in an array of colors, along with a cherry tree in full bloom; it took my breath away. There was a for sale sign in the yard, so I contacted the seller to see it. I was already sold on it because of the yard. There is definitely something to be said about the curb appeal.

I was able to see the house the same day and it was perfect for the three of us. I told the sellers that I wanted the house as long as the loan would work out. I was so excited to tell the girls so I called them, but, oh, my goodness, that did not go well. My youngest daughter was livid and that might be an understatement, she truthfully did not hardly speak to me for a year. There was so much anger and I didn't even know what to do with her. I tried to explain that there was no choice to keep her in the same school, but she wasn't hearing it. At twelve years old she just didn't get the whole finance thing and really didn't care. She was already so hurt by the divorce and our past history that I believe this was the tip of the iceberg. Her aching heart made me very sad.

My bubble was burst, the excitement was depleted, but I persevered as I had through every other disappointment and hurt throughout the years. With God all things are possible and I was learning that more and more.

God was definitely in this move. I went to my bank to see about a loan for the house. I already knew from becoming a mortgage loan officer, that I would not be able to get a regular mortgage because I had just recently started an all-commission job so guidelines would not allow it. There was such a kind man at the bank that proceeded to assist me and worked it out for me to get a loan to buy our new home. Only God could have made that happen.

I was doing a happy dance in my head and was elated with excitement. You see I was starting from the bottom. The abusive relationship that I had just come from had taught me that I amounted to nothing, as a result I had zero confidence. God was teaching me to lean on Him for all our needs. As we moved forward, there was a feeling of empowerment, that I could do anything with God's help. There was a sense of accomplishment and joy in having our own home. There was also a tremendous amount of responsibility that came with our new life, but God had me every step of the way.

The people I bought the house from were also part of God's plan. They were incredible and gracious. He would come back many times for the first year to show me how to work different things in the house. He had no obligation to do that. As a single woman, that was so helpful and reassuring. Thank you Lord for the believers you put in our path.

The first year of my job, I made thirteen thousand dollars along with the child support I was receiving. I can tell you, that on paper, there is no way that would have carried us that year to take care of my bills and other obligations, but God works in the supernatural. He was providing and making it work – more of my story of a journey of grace.

> *"And my God will meet all your needs according to the riches of his glory in Christ Jesus."*
>
> —Philippians 4:19

CHAPTER EIGHT

POINT OF SURRENDER

It was a ridiculously emotional phone call I made that night as I stood in the kitchen talking to the man I was sure would be my husband one day, it was a gut wrenching pain and sorrow I felt in my broken heart. God never said that surrendering the people and things that we love would be easy. The relationship with the guy that I was certain I loved, was not healthy for me. God was showing me that I was obsessed with him. I was the seductress in the relationship and the more he would pull away at times, I would insanely go after him. I would pray that he would marry me, I was completely out of my mind and thank the Lord for not answering my prayers.

The song, "Thank God for Unanswered Prayers" was popular at the time and it became my go-to song. God was so faithful to show me my heart and that I needed to surrender all of that dysfunctional relationship and look towards Him to receive what God had in store for me. The lights began to come on and wow, as joyful as I was to hear God and for my eyes to be opened, it was so hard to let go of someone that I thought I wanted so desperately to spend my life with. The irony in this is that my friend didn't have the same feelings I did. It was all me and my heart desires, not his. I know he cared, but he wasn't in a place in his heart to make any kind of commitment. I get that now.

Like it says in the song – "Amazing Grace! How sweet the sound that saved a wretch like me! I was once lost, but now am found, was blind but now I see."

I can only imagine that there might have been some angels singing hallelujah in the heavens, she is finally beginning to get it! Like the scriptures say about Saul's conversion, the scales were lifted from his eyes so he could see again. I believe that is what was happening to me. That time of surrender was a significant turning point in my life to move forward on a journey of grace with Jesus.

CHAPTER NINE

CREATING A NEW HEART

*"Create in me a clean heart, O God;
and renew a right spirit within me."*
—Psalms 51:10

That is exactly what God was beginning to do in my life. He had been patiently waiting for me to let go of the things that were holding me back from receiving the goodness He has had in store for me. I didn't realize it at the time but He was creating in me a new heart and spirit and it felt freeing. God never gave up on me.

God started me on a journey of learning my heart and passions that came only from Him. I had mentioned before that I had gone back to church and that is where God started speaking to me and revealing some of the spiritual gifts and passions He had created in me. I had no idea how I could serve Him. I would see others serving in a way that did not feel like anything I wanted to do, or that I felt capable of so what was I to do?

Our Pastor had announced an upcoming class to find out what our Spiritual Gifts were and I jumped on it, I was so curious. God had gotten my attention and I was hungry to be able to serve and pour my life into whatever He had in mind for me. The class was such an eye opener. I learned that a few of my gifts are encouragement, prayer, discernment and empathy. There may be a few more but these are the ones that stand out. We all have been given spiritual gifts. If you don't know what they are then I highly recommend that you find out. It made such a difference in my life. The places that I was able to use my gifts were not so evident. In knowing what my gifts were and what they meant helped me to begin to find the ministries where I could serve. There was more clarity therefore my frustrations diminished.

I have to mention a God thing that happened in that class. There were many people I did not know when I entered the room. I sat next to a woman, seeing her for the first time at this class. We immediately bonded, kindred spirits you might say. She became a lifelong soul sister in Christ! We have supported each other through some rough times and have made some wonderful memories.

The next opportunity that I heard about from our Pastor was something new he was starting. I heard him say, "if you are looking for some place to serve, then come and join me," so I said yes. I had no idea what it was about his invitation, but there was a nudge from God that said 'go.' As I look back on these times, it is so awesome how God was lining up all of these opportunities for me. He was so faithful in making sure that I had the tools to serve Him for the rest of my life. It just took me surrendering and saying yes without questioning.

I joined that group and what a journey it was. It was about learning how to facilitate small groups and support groups. I met many wonderful life friends there. We heard each other's hearts and life stories of brokenness and how each person was working through it with the help of Jesus. That was the first of many settings where God provided me the opportunity for healing. This group of friends surrounded me and listened to me share the pain and suffering that my children and I had just come from.

One of the friends from this group was a prayer warrior and he, with the help of Jesus, taught me how to pray. There was a day that we were leaving and I was standing in the parking lot with my friend. He knew there was something heavy on my heart so he stopped right where we were, dropped what he had in his hands, and began to pray for me. He will never know just how much of an impact that had on me. I learned something very important that day, to pray in the moment with those in need. You will learn later how instrumental he was in my most recent husband's life. He has truly been a blessing!

There was another friend from that group that serves with me today. Our daughters were best of friends growing up, but then we somewhat lost touch, until God prompted me to contact her later in years. We never know why God puts different people in our paths, but He definitely has a plan. He just asks us to trust Him.

After being trained to facilitate the groups I spoke about, I was called to lead a group on codependency. Previously, I had read a lot on codependency and many other self-help books. I was like a sponge, I wanted to get out of the stinking thinking that I had for so many years. I didn't want to be dysfunctional any more. I was reading everything I could get my hands on. All that I had read along with what I had learned in Al-anon and, with the help of Jesus, enabled me to climb out of that pit I had fallen into to take the path to a healthier me. I was ready to help others to do the same.

Author and Counselor Melodie Beattie explains codependency so well in her book, "Codependent No More." I have to say that when I read her book, I was sure she had written it about me. There is so much wonderful information in this book. I highly recommend it as a resource. Her work has made a positive impact on my life, but I am sure I will always struggle with some of these areas of codependency and breaking old patterns. I catch myself sometimes going back to that old self. I am thankful that I can be aware, and, through her teachings, be reminded of ways to create healthy relationships.

God has brought me so far, He has been trans-forming me throughout the years.

> *"O house of Israel, can I not do with*
> *you as this potter does?" declares*
> *the Lord. "Like clay in the hand of*
> *the potter, so are you in my hand, O*
> *house of Israel."*
>
> —Jeremiah 18:6

As my Sunday school class was ending one day, I heard the Lord say, "go start a single's class." The class I was participating in was all couples and I felt out of place, but was making the best of it until God spoke to me. It wasn't an audible voice, but a tap on the shoulder, and I just knew it was from God, not me.

I immediately went to our Pastor who was teaching the class and said to him, "I need a room to start a singles class." I am always in awe and was amazed then at how God moved and orchestrated through the entire conversation. There was never any hesitation or any questions asked by me or my Pastor. He said to start with his office while he found us another room.

We began to spread the word and before we knew it, we had regular attendance of 17 or so each week. We did this for a couple of years. We enjoyed Sunday class time and also we would have social events with other churches' singles groups.

Keep in mind that every time I heard God call me to serve, lead or facilitate a class or group, I had no idea what I was doing. I just heeded to the call and walked in faith. I was learning that He equips us with what we need and with God all things are possible.

> *"May the God of peace, who through the blood of the eternal covenant brought back from the dead our Lord Jesus, that great Shepherd of the sheep, equip you with everything good for doing his will, and may he work in us what is pleasing to him, through Jesus Christ to whom be glory forever and ever. Amen"*
> —Hebrews 13:20 & 21

There was a ministry in our church called Stephens Ministry. I didn't know anything about it other than hearing of them. One day one of the leaders reached out to me after hearing about the codependency group I was facilitating. She said that the leaders wanted me to come and teach on codependency to all of the Stephen Ministers for one of their continuing education classes. I was humbly honored, and a little nervous. This was brand new territory to me. Well, actually every-thing God was calling me to do was new and He continued to give me what I needed to serve where I was lead. After teaching that class, the same leader came to me a few days later to say that all of the leaders had prayed and they knew that I was to go to Stephens Ministry Leadership training.

Wow, that was overwhelming, and, the first time I really encountered someone telling me what they felt like God was telling them about me. I do love how God works, He is our sovereign God, all knowing and all wise. I was just learning about the ministry. It is for lay people going through 50 hours of training to become care-givers for those in crisis, to have a listening heart, to not counsel but to encourage and pray if the care receiver agrees to it. It is a powerful min-istry. God was really speaking to my heart and again revealing more opportunities that would enable me to use the gifts He had given me.

What was unusual about the request, that I go to leadership training first, as typically, a person would go through the 50 hours of training to become a Stephens Minister first, then go to the leadership training. It sounded like God wanted me to skip that step. Who was I to question Him? He had a plan.

My children were young, I was a single mom, and the training was in Orlando for two weeks. How in the world was I to pull that off? God had it, He provided a sitter to come to my house for two weeks so I could go. My mom and aunt were close by and the church paid my way, so I was off. That would be the first time I had gone away by myself to anything where I didn't know anyone. I will say that I heard from my children later that the sitter didn't work out so well and it really hurt my heart. I was thankful they were alive and well-nourished, but sad that there was something that took place that was a disadvantage to them. I am very sorry girls!

My soul sister's husband passed away unexpectedly a week before I was to go, she was so crushed and I didn't want to be anywhere but with her. It was so hard to leave, but I knew that is where God wanted me and that He was taking care of her. She and I learned over the years that sometimes He would separate us to cause us to lean on Him more and not each other. Learning to always put God first before any of those we love is a hard lesson but that is what He calls us to do.

The room where the training conference was held was full of about 400 people from all over the country and I didn't know a soul. It was a little much when I walked in that door, but quickly as I was assigned a table, I became friends with many wonderful people that loved Jesus. I was so humbled to be in that environment with so many like-hearted men and women. It was truly a gift from God. He was rebuilding me, my confidence and self-esteem, showing me who I was and that I was valuable to Him and others. (I had lost who I was in my previous marriage because of the abusive relationship). We worked long, hard days and into the nights at the conference. There was so much to learn about leading other Stephen Ministers and how to be one myself. A lot of it was coming natural to me because God wired me that way. I do not boast about this but will boast about the hard road I have been on to enable God to use all of it for His glory. He was equipping me and teaching me more skills, sharpening what I already had to do His will and this was just the beginning.

> *"Three times I pleaded with the Lord to take it away from me. But he said to me, "My grace is sufficient for you, for my power is made perfect in weakness." Therefore I will boast all the more gladly about my weaknesses, so that Christ's power may rest on me. That is why, for Christ's sake, I delight in weaknesses, in insults, in hardships, in persecutions, in difficulties. For when I am weak, then I am strong."*
>
> —2 Corinthians 12: 8-10

Several days went by when I met a young man to whom I was extremely attracted. Oh goodness, I thought that was all over. I had let go of the lustful, sinful nature of mine from years past, and here was truly a temptation from the enemy, right in the middle of this wonderful place like heaven where God had sent me.

That is just like Satan to show up at a time like that. I was so engrossed in learning and bathing in the Holy Spirit that the enemy blindsided me. I spent some time with this really attractive and kind young man. He was a youth leader at his church. We just never know who Satan will use to tempt us. I also learned that this guy was married. There were several days of conversation and spending time together in my room. I have always been so thankful to our Lord for giving him the courage and strength to say no to anything that would hurt either of us or others that we would be so full of shame. It was apparent that God surely had more work to do with me. I loved Jesus so much, but the flesh was still getting in the way.

The end of the two weeks was upon us. There was a commissioning for all of the new leaders and that event was one of the most humbling moments I have ever had. As we stood before those that were performing the ceremony, I had the feeling of being so small as I stood before the Lord to receive something that only He could give me, GRACE! I imagined for a minute how the disciples must have felt when called by Jesus. They, like me, were just ordinary, sinful people getting through life the best they could. Jesus Christ called them to serve Him and with Him. I was so emotional, my life flashed before my eyes with all the things I had done that would disappoint Jesus and I knew that I did not deserve to be standing before Him in that room, I did not deserve to be called to minister for Him and I didn't earn it. My journey of grace continues!

> *"For it is by grace you have been saved, through faith – and this not from yourselves, it is the gift of God – not by works, so that no one can boast."*
>
> —Ephesians 2:8, 9

CHAPTER TEN

GOD'S GRACES

He was stalking me! It was the guy who had been attending our singles Sunday school class for a while. He found out that I was at the conference center where they would have a singles night. I loved to dance so I was there every week. I began to notice that he would show up most of those nights for just a few minutes. I would spot him watching me and then he would vanish. One night, I actually caught up with him and after some conversation he agreed to ride with me to pick up my youngest daughter. I wasn't really attracted to him but there began to be something underlying that I couldn't explain. We began to get to know each other a little more outside our class.

One Friday morning a very close friend of mine that worked with this guy ran into him and learned that a couple of his daughters had cancelled going to dinner with him that night so she convinced him to ask me out. I heard from him late that morning. He said that he had made dinner reservations at a nearby restaurant and would I like to join him. I had previously surrendered to Jesus and finally for many months was at a place of contentment in my heart with my love for the Lord, to focus on serving Him, raising my girls, working on my career and not be in any more relationships, if that was what God willed.

Well, I did accept the dinner invitation and we had a fabulous evening! He swept me off my feet in just three hours. Jesus was blindsiding me with a relationship I never dreamed possible. Through the months of surrender, I would pray that yes, Jesus, I am content and will continue to be, if there is never to be another life partner but if it is in your will, I would pray that He would be preparing my heart for a man and a gentleman's heart for me. I asked Him to provide someone that would pray and worship with me, love Jesus as I did, and put Jesus in the center of our relationship.

God was blessing me with more than I could ever imagine. It was a whirlwind, we were spending every minute that we could with one another, talking about our faith and beliefs, our values, how we like to raise children, how we live life, what was important to us, finances, etc. We even learned that we both like to play bridge; we loved the game. We covered a lot of territory in a short period of time.

One evening, we were at a gazebo nearby and out of his mouth came the words "I love you". That was just two weeks from our first date. I felt that my feelings might be the same, but how could I feel that way so soon? I told him that he would have to give me some time. It scared me because of all that I had come through. It felt so right though. We were equally yoked, we both loved Jesus and our hearts had bonded spiritu-ally, we just knew. After a few days I admitted that I loved him and life was out of control after that. We decided to get married almost three months later. Together, we would pray over what we were about to do. I was like a teenager all over again! I was so giddy and happy, full of a joy that I just never experienced before. My heart was overflowing with Jesus' blessings. I couldn't contain myself; I wanted to shout from the rooftops about the love God had sent me.

My friends and family were not as excited as I was, they actually thought I had lost my mind, but they all supported me and trusted in what I said I had found in my new relationship. Funny thing is that my fiancé was nothing like I had ever been attracted to before. He was kind of a nerd, way too smart for me, he didn't like to dance (I would tell him later, that was his only flaw that I could see), his looks were not what I typically would be drawn to, either.

What I was learning is that it is the inside (the heart), of a man that was the most important. He loved me with his whole heart just as Jesus loves us. He loved me unconditionally and didn't care about what I had been in the past. He was a gentle man and had a great sense of humor. Everyone loved him, he never met a stranger and always made others feel welcome. There wasn't anything he couldn't do around the house. He honored me in a way that I felt so loved and cherished all the time. He was kind, selfless and had a servant's heart. I loved his voice and how he would call me "Love". God had been waiting to give me this beautiful gift and I will always be so humbly thankful to have had the opportunity to experience that kind of relationship. Not only was Jesus my rock, now this man, who would become my husband, was my earthly rock.

He and I were elated about making wedding plans, but there were some that were not so happy about it. He had three girls and I had two, and they didn't even know we were dating, much less making wedding plans. I am going to stop right here and make a disclaimer about the next steps in our lives. We all have a different perspective, and our own stories, about how this wedding stuff played out and then on to blending a family. I do recognize that, but I will tell it from my perspective. I know all of our girls may have something very different to say.

Once we decided to get married, we made the decision to live in my house and put an addition on, so off to the bank we went to get a loan and find a builder to get started. I was so much more anxious about co-signing a loan with my husband-to-be than getting married. I told him that if he backed out, he would always be obligated to the loan. My husband's youngest daughter was going to live with us until she graduated from high school; that was the reason for the addition.

My husband called his middle daughter and it went something like this... he asked her to come home to meet her future step-mom and try on her bridesmaid's dress. Goodness, can you imagine being her on the other end of that phone call? I have to say as we shared with each of our girls about our plans they were more gracious to our face than I had expected, but I know inside, their feelings did not reflect what they were portraying to us.

There was the issue around the green dress I wanted them to wear in the wedding. My youngest daughter kicked and screamed about it all the way to the wedding and I still hear about it occasionally today. We can laugh about it now. We had a long way to go with blending a family, but we knew that we would work through it with the help of Jesus.

The wedding was beautiful, we had about 150 friends and family there at our church. The reception afterward was so much fun and everything that we wanted. Many of my girlfriends pitched in to provide all the food and the cake and I will forever be grateful. It was a blast and I had never been so happy. It felt like I was in a dream. We were off to an amazing honeymoon for a few days then back home to reality to start a new life together with our blended family.

The first mistake we had made was leaving three of the girls at home while we were away. We learned that a couple of them had skipped school and the other had signed their permission slips. It was the beginning of some definite challenges in pulling our families together, much less raising teenagers. My husband's youngest and my youngest didn't care for one another in the beginning, but after some time they became best of friends and still are today. After getting to know his youngest better, I love and adore her and the relationship we have developed over time. After they moved out, they ended up rooming together while commuting to school. That was a true blessing.

There was a time early in our marriage that my husband and I thought it would be a good idea to have a family meeting. We were waiting on his youngest daughter to get home. My oldest got tired of waiting and just walked out the door. We really never had our meeting. My husband was a little put out that my daughter left, so he thought he was supporting me by putting a note on her door to say she was being disrespectful – or, something like that. Ok, that didn't go well, at all, either.

My daughter came home after he had gone to bed. I was doing laundry when she found the note on her door. She came over to me and threw it at me and said that he had no right. She was very angry and resentful. She would not speak to my husband for several weeks. He was persistent though and would come home for lunch every day hoping to catch her. He wanted to work out the relationship with her and after some time, it happened, they worked through it and they became really close.

She would call him dork, which was her word of affection for him because she didn't want to disrespect her father to call him dad. He began to call her the same and they did that for the rest of his life. He would end up being the loving, earthly father that neither she, nor my other daughter, had ever experienced. He was such a blessing for our family, I am not sure he ever knew just how much.

My husband and I had agreed from the beginning when there were decisions to be made around the girls, we would take it behind closed doors and pray about it. The parent then would deliver the decision. Our girls didn't like that very much. My youngest daughter would bring up that I had been making decisions on my own so why did I need him to help me now. There were so many changes for them but we stuck to our initial decisions in how to blend the family. We stood up for what we believed and did our best not to let any of the girls play us against the other. We put Jesus first, then each other, then the children.

That is what God's word calls us to do in a family unit. It was not always easy. There were some angry and resentful girls sometimes, and definitely some rebellion. Our hearts hurt for each of them at times as we went through the changes. We never wanted to drive any of our children away from us. The girls didn't fall in love with me or him, they didn't ask for this new family, they were not given a choice. God had worked through those years to transform us to a loving, blended family.

My husband loved each of his girls so much and was so proud of who they had become. He would light up when he spoke of all of the girls. We were always, and I am still, so proud of each of our girls – and, I include my girl's half-sister that I mentioned previously in another chapter. My husband embraced her and her family to include them in our clan. In my youth when I said I never wanted children, I would never have imagined the plans God had for a family for me. He has blessed me with my two beautiful girls and four beautiful stepdaughters that I love as my own and their spouses. I am so blessed to have been able to share their lives. They have given me ten wonderful grandchildren, eight girls and two boys. I am eternally grateful for my relationship with every one of you. I love you all so much.

My husband and I had such an amazing, Godly relationship. I had all that I could have ever asked for. We prayed and worshipped together. He was my soul mate, my person, my confidant and my best friend. I never knew what it was like to be honored until he came along. For once, I had a healthy relationship and it was all centered on Jesus. He is who makes us whole, not our mates or anyone else. We have to be whole in our hearts with Jesus Christ. We cannot depend on any one person to do that for us. Jesus is the only way.

"Jesus answered, "I am the way and the truth and the life. No one comes to the Father except through me."
—John 14:6

We loved to travel and be with friends. We were blessed to meet a couple early on in our marriage that ended up being our travel companions for many wonderful years and we had a blast with them. I love the memories that we have made together. I will always cherish them. They were our closest couple friends. We were blessed with many other friends throughout the years. He and I loved being with other people or we could be perfectly happy just sitting on the couch hand in hand. We never lost our affection for one another. I am pretty sure we embarrassed our girls sometimes. We told each other many times a day I love you. The best thing in the world was his hugs. They made me feel so secure. I would love to have one of them today.

We were fortunate to be able to provide several family vacations and what memories they are. It was so much fun playing horseshoes, sharing the cooking of meals, playing games, hanging out on the beach, and just being with one another.

There was so much laughter and happiness. Thank you Jesus for those times of experiencing a blended family enjoying one another. It is a precious memory I will cherish forever. If I could only turn back the time and do it again!

Our relationship was easy because we loved each other as Jesus loves us. We were not perfect, but I have to say that the only serious argument we may have ever had was over a silly trashcan. It just worked for us and we were so blessed. One thing that probably drove my husband crazy is that every night before we would say goodnight I would turn to him and ask him about his day, check on his heart, and was there anything that was bothering him about our relationship, family or life in general.

That was the Stephens Minister in me, but since he was so gracious with me, he would answer those questions and I would talk about how I might be feeling also. We then would read through a devotion every night, then pray out loud about the things we had discussed and then off to sleep. I will tell you that was the most special times of our day. I learned that it was much more intimate than any love making we could have ever had. I believe that is why we had such a strong marriage, and why I believe it is so important for every couple to pray aloud together. There is a vulnerability and transparency that takes place that is quite humbling. We humble ourselves before our Father and our marriage partner at the same time. We shouldn't hide any feelings from the other, be honest with your loved one. I believe there is a lot of respect that comes out of it.

My husband was so amazing at supporting me in hard times. My dad, whom I adored and loved so much, suddenly passed away after my husband and I had been married for four years. I was a daddy's girl. We had such a fun relationship. He was always there for me and rescued me when I was in trouble. He loved me unconditionally.

There was a time that I had announced in my young adult life that I was living with a guy outside marriage. My mom was so hurt and angry that she disowned me and told me to leave and never come back, that I was no longer her daughter! I was driving a car of my dad's at the time because he was a car dealer, so he was always providing a car to me. Yes, I might have been a little spoiled! She told me to take the car back to my dad the next morning and she didn't care how I got to work after that.

My dad was hurt about my announcement but continued to love me and didn't say a word. The next day, I returned my car to him and a friend drove me to work. Within a couple of days, my dad showed up with a car for me to purchase for forty-nine dollars a month. This was in nineteen seventy four so it is all relative, but I know now that he probably carried most of the cost for that car. He was making sure I was taken care of even though he did not approve of what I was doing. Don't you know that is what God does for us? He is always watching over us and has our best interest at heart, He loves us unconditionally and provides for us even though we don't deserve it and at times when we don't even realize it. What an amazing God I serve.

I learned from the experience of my mom disowning me how important it is to extend grace at a time we don't approve or agree with something our loved one does. I knew she wasn't going to be happy about it but never dreamed she would respond that way. Later in life, I would remember to use that experience towards our children even though we might be angry with their actions.

My dad's death sent me in to several years of depression, panic and anxiety. I didn't know how to do life without him. When I received the call from my step-mom that he had been taken to the hospital, we took off across the city to get to him. I was anxious, not knowing what to expect. We got there too late.

I was taken into a room where my oldest daughter and husband were. Someone came in to tell me that dad had passed away, I went to my knees screaming out in

gut– tormenting pain in my heart. He had been taken away from me and I didn't get to say goodbye, just as it had been when my brother passed away. My youngest daughter and I chose to go to see his body but when we got to the door and looked in, he was purple and it just didn't look like him – I just couldn't go any closer. He had died from a common food bacteria and it had caused his body to change colors. My stepmom was by his side, I was so sorry for her. They had only been married for five weeks after being together for seven years. Dad had waited patiently for her to say yes to marry him. I am so thankful that his dream came true before he left this earth to go be with our Heavenly Father.

The days turned into months, then years of the deep depression I was suffering from. My husband was a saint, he tolerated me and encouraged me, and he loved and supported me. He would hold me in his arms night after night as I cried myself to sleep.

> *"How long, Lord? Will you forget me forever? How long will you hide your face from me? How long must I wrestle with my thoughts and day after day have sorrow in my heart? How long will my enemy triumph over me? Look on me and answer, Lord, my God. Give light to my eyes, or I will sleep in death, and my enemy will say, "I have overcome him," and my foes will rejoice when I fall. But I trust in your unfailing love; my heart rejoices in your salvation. I will sing the Lord's praise, for he has been good to me.*
>
> —Psalms 13:1-6

It became difficult for me to go outside and to drive out of our community. I was imprisoned in my panic and anxiety. I was like a kid looking through a window at those outside playing but not being able to join them. I was frozen and couldn't move in my mental state that I was in. If you have been there, you know what it feels like. I just wanted to sleep it off and wanted it to go away. I only had my mom left in my immediate family now. Because of her pain and hurt she went through after my parent's divorce, she had come to me after my dad passed away to say she could not be there for me, so within my immediate family unit there was no one to talk to about my dad so I carried it deep in my soul.

Even though I was in so much turmoil, I could see through the tunnel that there was light at the other end, there was hope because I knew and had faith in my God who loves me and promises me his faithfulness. Deep down, I was looking forward to seeing what God would do with all that I was going through, there was joy in my heart in the midst of the suffering.

> *"I remember my affliction and my wandering, the bitterness and the gall. I well remember them, and my soul is downcast within me. Yet this*

I call to mind and therefore I have hope: Because of the LORD's great love we are not consumed, for his compassions never fail. They are new every morning; great is your faithfulness. I say to myself, "The LORD is my portion; therefore I will wait for him."

—Lamentations 3:19-24

God was restoring me a little at a time as I continued to worship Him, serve Him and walk with Him. Family life got better and we were enjoying life with one another. With all that we were going through, it never seemed to affect our marriage, God was keeping us strong and we were always turning to Him for guidance.

My youngest daughter was probably about 15 or so when we had an encounter that would begin a transformation in her. I have mentioned earlier in this book about her being a strong-willed child. Well, that is just part of the story. From a very young age, she was super rebellious towards me. If I said it was black, she said it was white. She never liked any clothing I picked out for her, she blamed me for anything that happened to her. She was always arguing with me about anything. I had mentioned before that it was a love/hate relationship. She was so helpful and could fix anything, even when she was really young, I was amazed. She was mechanical and resourceful and still is to this day. She wasn't my affectionate one, but she didn't want to get too far from me, either. She was attached to my hip. I put her in preschool at three years of age, she cried for the first two months, so I had to take her out. She was a hard child to raise, but I know now that in order to be strong and courageous as she is, she had to test the world, including me.

In my daughter's defense, she desperately wanted to be a daddy's girl. She had disappointment after disappointment by her father. She always was putting her hope in him and every time he would break her heart. She had it rough growing up. Most of his verbal abuse was put on her. With that being said, as she moved into the adolescence stage of her life, she had lost all of her confidence and self-esteem. She began to run with the wrong circle of friends and was making bad choices. Eventually, I could look into her eyes and see darkness in her soul. The enemy had taken over her body. She had a best friend (I called them partners in crime), that she got in trouble with many times. My heart cried for her. I prayed daily for God to rebuke Satan out of her, to bring her back to life. I wanted God to take control of her. My reactions to her behavior was not so healthy either. We would scream at each other. The second time my husband came to pick me up when we were dating, he heard us when we were standing in her bedroom screaming at the top of our lungs. It is amazing that he stayed around after that. That was not good parenting on my part. I had never learned how not to react to her in a way that didn't send me spiraling. Now I know that I should have responded in a soft, loving way to stop the noise. Sometimes we learn too late, but we can pass it on to others and our adult children.

My daughter had gotten to the place where she had no remorse for anything that she did. She really had become an unruly child in our home and it wasn't fair to the other children. No matter what discipline we tried or what I said to her, there was nothing that would make a difference. I had come to a place where even though I loved her with all of my heart I didn't like who she had become. I couldn't stand to be around her. She was not the person that God had created, Satan had control of her and I was ready to put a stop to it or at least be done with her behavior in our home. One particular day, I got word that her friend had been picked up by the police at school as an unruly child because of something they had both done. I called my husband and asked if he would come home early before the other children. I went to the school and picked up my daughter and brought her home. We sat her down and drenched in tears, I began to say to her that she was no longer welcome to live in the house with us, it didn't matter to me whether she went to juvenile, a foster home, or to her dads, but she could not live with us anymore and said to her that she had a choice to make right then.

I had surrendered to the fact that I was ready to let her go. I could not get any control over her life so now it was all up to God. It was the hardest conversation I had ever had. Within the moment, something changed, I knew in my heart of hearts that she had made a positive choice to change and I believe in an instant once I surrendered her life, God took over and removed the enemy from her. It was so unbelievable because her pattern would say differently, but the Holy Spirit moved into that room to begin a life transformation in my daughter.

Today, she is an amazingly beautiful and smart young woman of God. She is a hard worker as an accounting manager and gets the single mom award, as far as I am concerned. She is always there to support her friends and walk alongside them in times of trouble. She is the first to be by my side if I need her and I am so very proud of who she has become and in awe of what God can do with all of us. God was waiting on me to surrender. He often has told me through the years to not interfere in His journey with my children. He has been growing and transforming them in ways that I could never. Turning my children over to Him has been very hard for me and I haven't been perfect at it but He reminds me often. God is an awesome God and all things are possible with Him. He answered my prayers. It took a long time, but during the process of waiting on God, He was teaching me and sifting me, as He continues to do.

This was another time that my husband was so faithful in supporting me. He certainly saw me shed a lot of tears and he never left my side. I am so thankful to God for sending a man who loved me and our daughters like he did. He was there for my daughter and helped me to encourage her as she moved forward. I began to see light in her eyes and a smile on her face. It was baby steps but she was and has been transforming into who God created her to be. It is and has been a process as it is for all of us. She went on to college and graduated with honors. Before, she didn't care about school or her grades but I always knew she was ridiculously smart. I mentioned earlier in the book about her having a child and raising her in the church, teaching her to love Jesus. I continue to be in awe of our loving Father as He has been sifting my youngest for a long time and I see the beautiful creation she is turning into and I can't wait to see how He continues to use her life for the good of others. It has been an honor to witness such a beautiful testimony of which I am confident, that one day she will be sharing her story.

My husband's youngest daughter is married and has a beautiful daughter. My stepdaughter was a daddy's girl and my husband thought she hung the moon. About 10 or 11 years ago, my stepdaughter and her husband moved out to Washington State, the other side of the country from us. That was hard for me and my husband, but especially for him. They were very close and had a special relationship. She has been diligent and worked really hard to get to where she is today and I am so proud of her for all that she has accomplished and love her dearly. She currently is an Environmental Planner for the State of Washington. I have had the pleasure to be able to visit several times since they have been gone. I always love and adore the time I get to spend with her, her husband, and my granddaughter.

Unlike many high school graduates, my oldest daughter and her friend decided to go half way around the world on a mission trip for two months, in the fall after their senior year. That was a huge leap of faith and a little unnerving. The only way we could communicate with them was by fax and it was close to a month before I heard from her, other than knowing they had made it safely. It was such a good feeling to get her back home and when she came back, I knew she was different, that God was calling her to go out into the world to be a disciple of nations. There was no stopping her and I didn't want to, but I had to pray a lot because it was scary for me. She went off to college, then became involved in a mission ministry called Global Scope, an organization that plants campus ministries at universities all over the world. She had found her passion and has such a love for young people. She and her husband sold everything they owned and took off to Mexico for five years, where two of my grandchildren were born.

They, along with another couple, planted a campus ministry at UDLA in Puebla, Mexico. She continues her ministry in Alabama, currently as a camp director for a missionary camp. I sometimes think of what Mary, Jesus Christ's mother, must have felt loving a son that loved His mission more. I am so humbled for what my daughter does, but if I am honest, it has been hard sometimes because I know that her love for God and what He calls her to do is first in her life – even as it should be. Mary stood by and watched her son, the Savior of the world, go out among the people to minister and put His mission first before His family. It takes a lot of faith to be able to let go of your family member and to really understand that he or she belongs to God first and is a gift to us. There have been times that I have selfishly longed for her to be close to home again so that I can spend more time with her and her family. Then I am reminded that she is focusing on walking in the will of God, our entire purpose for our journey on this earth.

My husband's middle daughter has always been gracious and diplomatic with us. I love her visits when she is in town. I have had the pleasure to go and visit her in different locations where she would be stationed. She has served our country in the Air Force for about 20 years and has done it well. She has worked extremely hard to achieve her accomplishments and now is a Colonel, and I am so proud of her. Thank you for serving! My husband was always so interested in where she was and what she was doing. She has been all over the world. He would hang on to every word she said and loved to tell others about her. I remember when he learned while she was in college that she was joining the ROTC. He was so surprised but what a blessing that she knew early in life what she wanted to do. He loved her and was extremely proud. Also, she has done a beautiful job helping to raise her stepdaughter.

My husband's oldest daughter is another one that gets a single mom award. She has parented her three beautiful girls as a single mom, for most of their life, and I have been so inspired by her and how she has gotten through some hard times. She has so much of her dad's gentle spirit. She has worked very hard to get where she is today and now has a great job working as a marketing manager for the company where her dad worked for years. It is kind of awesome as though she has come full circle and the people there adore her as they did her father. Her dad was so proud of her and loved her dearly. He loved his time with her, they had similar interests in building and creating things. I think she can do just about anything with her hands, just the same as her father.

God began to show me the meaning of grace in a profound way when my husband and I went to a "Walk to Emmaus" Christian retreat. My husband went the first weekend and I the second. He already loved Jesus, but when he came home I saw a changed man. He wasn't able to tell me what to expect from the weekend, but he was giddy. It was so funny to see him like that, he was like a little kid that had found this treasure and wanted to share it so badly. He was so sweet and was anxious for me to go on my weekend. I have never experienced love (agape love), like I did those three days. Everywhere we turned, we were being loved on. It was as though I had met Jesus for the first time. There was no judgment, no condemnation, just pure love. It was a very emotional time, a time of growth and healing. Everyone received something different from the retreat but GRACE was big for me. I began to understand what real grace looks like. Grace, God's divine influence in the human heart and it's reflection on it, with thankfulness. Looking back, I know now that God was preparing me to be able to recognize the journey of grace I would experience in situations that we would encounter in the coming years.

> *"Grace and peace be yours in abundance through the knowledge of God and of Jesus our Lord."*
> —2 Peter: 1, 2

CHAPTER ELEVEN

OUR WORLD
WAS ROCKED

"The doctor will see you now in the family room," they said! Your husband has CANCER, the doctor announced. *No...you must be making a mistake.* We were told that there was probably no cancer and the lump just needed to be removed. I was all alone and hearing this news sent me spiraling. Our world had been rocked, all the dreams and plans we had made were vanishing before my eyes. There was no one with me. I don't believe I have ever felt as alone as I did in that moment! I wanted to run, I wanted to scream out. I needed someone's shoulders to cry on before I would see my husband.

How was I going to share the news with the girls? What was I to do?

It was four hours before I was able to see him, which seemed like an eternity; his tongue had swollen and they were watching him closely. He couldn't be released from recovery until the swelling had gone down. I began to call our family and many of our friends to share what I had been told. I was asking for prayers for it is the most powerful action we can take for those that are suffering. Finally, I was lead to the room where he would be admitted. As I was headed down the hallway, there was a chaplain speaking throughout the hospital over their speaker praying for all of medical staff and patients. I am convinced that was God showing up for me in a powerful way to remind me that He was in control and He was ever-present, pouring out His love, mercy and grace over us. He knew exactly what I needed at the time, to pull my focus back on Him.

In March of that year, my husband's tongue was becoming numb, but he sort of ignored it, as he said men have a way of doing. Then he realized that when he ate, there was a lump swelling under his jaw. That got his attention. He went to an ENT and was treated as though it were an infection in his saliva gland. He was given antibiotics, but it wasn't helping. He then went back to the doctor and it was decided that he would have a biopsy done in the doctor's office. It was inconclusive for cancer. The doctor wasn't convinced though and requested to schedule surgery to remove the saliva gland.

This was just prior to my youngest daughter's wedding, so my husband decided to schedule after the wedding was over so her plans would not be interrupted. That was how he was, always thinking of others. We were told that it would be just a one day and night stay in the hospital. It was way on the other side of Atlanta from where we live so I decided to pack a bag and stay with him and return home the next day. Any of those that have known me for years, know that I do not like driving across Atlanta so that was an easy solution for me.

Once I received the news of cancer, I learned there was going to be many more nights in the hospital. I was waiting in my husband's room when they finally brought him in. I have to tell you that I was bracing myself for what I was about to see. They had removed two saliva glands and

25 lymph nodes, so I couldn't even imagine what he was going to look like. I was pleasantly surprised (kind of an odd statement I guess). They did a really good job on his neck. His neck was glued rather than stitching or staples. What I didn't like was the feeding tube that was inserted in his nose. He was not able to have any food or drink, not even a piece of ice in his mouth. My empathetic heart did not handle that very well. The only way he could get any moisture was by moving a wet sponge on a stick around in his mouth. Keep in mind that he had lost two of his saliva glands, so the built-in natural moisture had been decreased.

I never left his side through the next five days of his stay in the hospital. I was longing for some of our support system to come and they began to show up. It was so good to see others that loved my husband and me. It would be the beginning of really having an understanding of what it meant and the importance to have a Christian community of support. My daughter and new son-in–law got off the airplane from their honeymoon and came straight to the hospital; it was so good to see them. I was missing family. My youngest stepdaughter had to bring more clothes to me because I was not leaving. I was so thankful to see her and to have some help with her dad. I slept on a recliner that wouldn't stay reclined for four nights – it was a battle every night. My husband was on morphine for the pain so he was awake every couple of hours. I learned the last night that they could have brought a mattress in for me to sleep on, really I thought, that would have been so nice to know earlier. There was no rest for the weary. I know that God designed us to have adrenalin to run on in a time of crisis and I ran on it for years. I had to lean on God and rest in Him.

> *"Come to me, all you who are weary and burdened, and I will give you rest. Take my yoke upon you and learn from me, for I am gentle and humble in heart, and you will find rest for your souls. For my yoke is easy and my burden is light."*
> —Matthew 11: 28-30

It was time for my husband to be released. (I have recently been reading through his journal in preparation for writing about his illness), He said, and I quote, "the doctor finally discharged me after I got instructions on how to feed myself with the syringe by pumping the Ensure in my nasal tube. At least I did not have to taste the stuff!"

He was always looking for something positive in the midst of what he was going through. He made me laugh.

The ride home was very emotional. We had many talks in the hospital about what life might look like after the diagnosis. We both agreed that the Lord was going to do great things through this journey and that our faith was about to be deepened more than we could imagine. It may be hard to understand, but we were excited to see what God would do as we embarked on the journey of cancer. It broke my heart to think of what my husband might have to experience, we had no idea what was to come. We called all of our daughters on the way home, my husband talked to them while I was driving. It was emotional for him to talk to them about his diagnosis. We were always so thankful for such loving girls. It was really hard for them to hear and I know that the ones that did not get to come to the hospital had struggled with not being able to see him. We continued to make calls during our drive to so many friends and family. As my husband said, "I am sure we forgot some and I am sorry, but it was not like we had a list – I should have, being an engineer and all."

Coming home looked quite different, we had so many new adjustments to make and were waiting for further test results, doctor appointments and how to move forward in our life. Right away we began to receive a multitude of cards and calls, visits from people and prayers from those we love. I am so thankful for the community that God puts in our lives. The Saturday after we came home, my husband wrote; "It was this day that I first met with my new spiritual mentor, he likes to think of himself as Obie Wan Kanobi, but I see him more as Yoda."

From that day forward, my husband always called our dear friend and his spiritual mentor, Yoda. I was walking out of my bedroom and glanced in the sunroom where Yoda and my husband were standing and I saw something that almost broke me. The two were embraced as my husband cried out uncontrollably in pain, and for what might be coming in the days ahead. I heard my husband say that if he had to die from this disease to bring someone to Jesus Christ, he would surrender!

> *"Father, if you are willing, take this cup from me; yet not my will, but yours be done."*
> —Luke 22:42

It was everything I could do to keep from falling apart. That scene will forever be planted in my brain. It was the beginning of an amazing relationship that only God could ordain. Our friend meant more to my husband than he will ever know. God used him to mentor, to encourage, to bring scripture to him, to bring fellowship to him and to pray for him. I had met this friend in a group back in the earlier days at church – he is the one I said had taught me how to pray. I am forever grateful, my friend, for all you have done for us.

Prayers were already being answered as God was circling us with our Christian community. I was concerned about being able to work and how I was going to get my husband to treatments. Within 24 hours, I had a call from one of my husband's friends to say that he and many guys from their Log House group would help to drive him. When my husband was out of work for so long, he was able to start attending the Men's Log House group (a group of praying and Jesus-loving guys who met in the community Log House building). I was so thankful for them. When my husband was not able to attend the meetings, they would come to him. I would look outside on Friday mornings and here comes car after car, lined up in front of my house, as the guys came to minister and visit with him. Also, my husband's close friends from the Emmaus group were ready and available. One of the guys from our church began to show up every week to cut our grass without any discussion. I had a woman from our church begin to show up outside of my house and sit on a bench to pray for us. Four of my closest friends were at my beckon call and checking on me all the time. We had our small group from church who was always checking in and praying for us. My mom made sure we had food along with others if I would let them. My aunt was a praying woman so she was all over us in prayer along with an incredibly strong prayer warrior circle. Cards, notes and encouraging phone calls flooded our home. My mom, step-dad and his family, our girls and their families and my husband's sister and brother in law were all there for us, not to mention so many wonderful friends. We were so humbled with emotions and thanksgiving. I have never known so much grace and love as we experienced throughout our journey.

We began to settle in and adjust for the few days of the nasal feeding tube while we waited for his doctor appointment for results and to learn what was next. He finally got the feeding tube out before seeing the oncologist. The day of the appointment came and off we went. We met the oncologist for the first time and he shared with us the results, it was not good at all. We learned that he had Stage 4 Squamous Cell Cancer in his saliva glands and that it had spread into some of his lymph nodes. They were not really sure where it originated. The doctor proceeded to tell us that the type of cancer he had was extremely rare so he was going to consult with many other doctors at a conference to determine the protocol for treatments.

The doctor told us that my husband would be doing chemo and radiation treatments simultaneously. He had to have a head brace made to fit him at the radiation center. He went without me when it was to be fitted for him. The first time that he was to have his radiation treatment, I went with him. I walked into the room where they lay him on a table and bolted this head brace down to the table over his entire head, it looked like a mask out of some horror movie. I am very claustrophobic, so let me tell you that was the worst thing I have ever seen and it made me sick to my stomach. I had to walk out of the room, I couldn't stand seeing him like that. My heart cried for him.

My husband was amazing, he never complained, he complied at every level just to get through all that he was to encounter. When doing both chemo and radiation in the same time period, one exacerbates the other so it was a horrible time for him. His neck was getting so burned that it looked like his neck had been laid across a charcoal grill, his neck had a third degree burn and he was miserable. I cried many tears over his pain and suffering. Consequently, it was time to give him a stomach feeding tube. It was such a pain to deal with, but it really was a God send at the time. He wasn't able to swallow and not only was his neck and throat burned, but now he had Thrush in his mouth and he was not able to put anything through his mouth. By having the feeding tube, we were able to get all of his medicine and nutrition in him to try and keep up his strength. My husband loved all kinds of food, he missed being able to taste all of his favorites. Eventually, when he would be able to eat again, his taste buds were always changing. The chemo would give him a metal taste or something else. Food never tasted the same again.

We learned that two more of my husband's saliva glands had been destroyed from the radiation so now he couldn't really make any of his own saliva, his mouth was always dry, and it was such a challenge for him. My husband had endured much already and it was far from over. One day he was in one of his "poor me, why me" moments and he picked up a book that Yoda had given him called "Prison to Praise" by Merlin Carothers. It is a book of faith, healing and the power of the Holy Spirit. In the book, the Lord is speaking to the author, a Presbyterian minister. In his story, God is suggesting to the minister that any time something happens to him that is less difficult than what happened to Jesus, to be just as glad as when he was asked if he was glad that Christ died for him.

My husband's response to this statement was "WOW – doesn't that put my pain and problem in perspective." I was humbled by that statement and realize again how we all just need to praise Him and give Him all the glory and have our lives filled with joy."

I am so humbled to have his journal to reflect on and to remember how much my husband loved Jesus. When we were first married, I was so thankful to have a husband that wanted to worship and get to know Jesus with me. I had mentioned we attended a Walk to Emmaus retreat. It was just prior to him losing his job. I had the honor to witness an amazing spiritual growth in my husband from that time and while he was out of work. He started going to the Log House group and meeting with several brothers in Christ from the Emmaus walk. He would have never had that opportunity if he had not lost his job. I know all the timing was ordained by God. God was preparing him for his cancer journey to strengthen him spiritually so that he could walk with grace and know to keep his focus on our Lord and Savior Jesus Christ. God was using him as a testimony.

My husband had started back to work prior to starting his treatments. He hardly missed a day. He was persevering through life with God's help. After the 18 months of being unemployed, one of his dear friends offered him a job working with him. God was still orchestrating. His employer and his friend were both very kind and understanding, having compassion for what he was going through. Our friend who offered the job, as my husband said in his journal, has a huge heart, he just tries to hide it. He still has a huge servant heart and I will always be so grateful to you, my friend.

My husband, as I might have mentioned earlier, loved wood working. He had a workshop in our garage and many days he would disappear to his workshop and be creating something. It was great therapy for him and he did beautiful work. He had two very close friends that would come and hang in the workshop with him as they worked side-by-side building, creating and bonding. I would laugh at one of them, and my husband. They were like the odd couple. My husband was a perfectionist (an engineer, remember), and our friend, definitely not. My husband would come in the house sometimes and say he just couldn't watch his friend any more, he would say he wasn't doing it right). It would crack me up. The other friend was learning from my husband and was so engaged and committed to be able to build like him. His friend would tell you today that they weren't finished – he still had much to learn. My husband had so many wonderful Christian friends. It made my heart happy to see the bond with each one of them.

The round of treatments were finished and life was looking a little better, my husband was in remission and healing for several months. He was able to eat again even though food still didn't taste the same. His birthday was at the end of July and all he wanted was pancakes. It was a glorious day for him and us to watch him eat them. It's the little things that we take for granted. Those pancakes were a big deal to him.

Many of our girls and family would visit us through this time and the years to come. They will never know how much pleasure and joy they brought us by making their appearance. We looked forward to seeing them and were so thankful for the memories.

Our cancer journey was one of the most spiritual times we ever experienced together. We knew in the beginning of the diagnosis that it was going to be a journey for God. It was a ridiculously hard journey for both of us and we of course were coming from two different perspectives. When a family member is diagnosed with cancer, the whole family has cancer. It was hard on our girls and their families. We all walked in it differently. I cried more than I have in my whole life. I wanted my husband to survive the disease that I hate with a passion. I was in prayer daily and learned that the journey of life is not about us, but about our Heavenly Father. We are put here for one purpose only and that is to serve Him and glorify Him in everything we do.

> *"Not to us, Lord, not to us but to your name be the glory, because of your love and faithfulness."*
> —Psalm 115:1

The journey is to reach the ultimate, to spend eternity with God. The hard part is the suffering that we must endure in our life time. In my morning prayers, I would ask God to walk through the day with me to help me face whatever my husband was to encounter. I cannot go through anything without God. He is our Sovereign Lord and loves us so much. He knows best and He will comfort us and give us a peace that we can't acquire any other way. What a relief it is to know that we don't have to do it alone.

My husband's oldest daughter had emailed us this scripture and story that I want to share.

> *"Go down to the potter's house, and there I will give you my message."*
> —Jeremiah 18:2

THE TEACUP STORY

There was a couple who used to go to England to shop in the beautiful stores. They both liked antiques and pottery and especially teacups. This was their twenty-fifth wedding anniversary.

One day in this beautiful shop they saw a beautiful cup. They said, "May we see that? We've never seen one quite so beautiful."

As the lady handed it to them, suddenly the cup spoke. "You don't understand," it said. "I haven't always been a teacup. There was a time when I was red and I was clay. My master took me and rolled me and patted me over and over and I yelled out, 'let me alone,' but he only smiled, 'Not yet.'

"Then I was placed on a spinning wheel," the cup said, "and suddenly I was spun around and around and around. Stop it! I'm getting dizzy! I screamed. But the master only nodded and said, 'Not yet.'

"Then he put me in the oven. I never felt such heat!" the teacup said. "I wondered why he wanted to burn me, and I yelled and knocked at the door. I could see him through the opening and I could read his lips as He shook his head, 'Not yet.'

"Finally the door opened, he put me on the shelf, and I began to cool. "There, that's better," I said. And he brushed and painted me all over. The fumes were horrible. I thought I would gag. 'Stop it, stop it!' I cried. He only nodded, 'Not yet.'

"Then suddenly he put me back into the oven, not like the first one. This was twice as hot and I knew I would suffocate. I begged. I pleaded. I screamed. I cried. All the time I could see him through the opening, nodding his head saying, 'Not yet.'

"Then I knew there wasn't any hope. I would never make it. I was ready to give up. But the door opened and he took me out and placed me on the shelf.

One hour later he handed me a mirror and said, 'Look at yourself.' And I did. I said, 'That's not me; that couldn't be me. It's beautiful. I'm beautiful.'

"'I want you to remember, then,' he said, 'I know it hurts to be rolled and patted, but if I had left you alone, you'd have dried up.

I know it made you dizzy to spin around on the wheel, but if I had stopped, you would have crumbled.

I knew it hurt and was hot and disagreeable in the oven, but if I hadn't put you there, you would have cracked.

I know the fumes were bad when I brushed and painted you all over, but if I hadn't done that, you never would have hardened; you would not have had any color in your life.

And if I hadn't put you back in that second oven, you wouldn't survive for very long because the hardness would not have held.

Now you are a finished product. You are what I had in mind when I first began with you.'"

~ Author Unknown

One day my husband started to cough, it was enough that it alarmed us so he went to his primary doctor to check it out. I had gone to our Wednesday night dinner at church and planned to meet him there. He showed up after his appointment and I asked, "What did the doctor say?"

He was told that he had Pneumonia! I couldn't even believe what I was hearing. "Why are you here, why aren't you being admitted in the hospital?" I was frantic and concerned.

I was appalled that with his recent diagnosis that the doctor didn't send him straight to the hospital. I told him we were leaving and headed to the emergency room, which, by the way, would be one of many visits. We were there on a Friday afternoon so it took some time, but they finally admitted him to a room to treat him with antibiotics and help him get stronger.

We were there all weekend to wait on a pulmonary doctor to see him on Monday morning. His lungs were filling up with fluid and he was so uncomfortable. It's all that hurry up and wait stuff that you go through in a cancer journey. I learned to be more patient through that four years than I ever thought possible.

Finally, Monday came and the pulmonary doctor came to visit. He pulled several liters of fluid off of his lungs and had it biopsied. We soon learned that my husband had small cell cancer in the pleura of his lungs – here we go again with round two. It was not the same cancer that he had the first time. The pleura is the lining around the lungs.

There is no easy cancer, but he just couldn't get a break. This was another fairly rare location for the cancer. Because it was in the lining, there was nothing to remove surgically. He continued to have the fluid removed then the doctor suggested that he go to another hospital and have a procedure done that was like putting talcum powder around the lining so that the fluid would not continue to seep in. What an amazing blessing that they could do that. It stopped immediately.

It was time for more chemo treatments. He had a port put in this time. He was a trooper going through all of that again. He continued to work and do other activities that were important to him. Recently, my husband had actually taken another job. The company where he was working ended up shutting down. Now we were concerned that he would not be able to get another job because of being sick. He would have to start all over again.

Well, as God would have it, a job was put in his lap with a local company where the employer and others that worked there were all Christians. Our God is sovereign, He already knew what our needs were going to be and was providing for us. My husband ended up with a young man as a business partner to work with and he was such a blessing to my husband. They developed a strong relationship in Christ. He was always by his side to help.

We continued to worship the Lord and our faith was growing. My husband was such a precious man, I loved him so much. He inspired me and I was in awe of him every day. We both knew that this diagnosis was not good, our faith was strong but we knew that this could be a journey to end of life for him. We had a lot of conversations about what that might look like. He wanted to make sure I was taken care of. They were hard conversations, but necessary. He was not scared to die, but surely would have loved to hang around longer to see his family grow and experience life with all of us.

We had an opportunity to travel to Cabos San Lucas for a week vacation with a couple we had known for just a little while. I was really concerned about leaving the country, not knowing what that would be like if he ended up having to go to the hospital again. It scared me, but he was insistent. It was important to him, so I prayed and agreed to go, surrendering it all to God. I had no control.

Off we went to a beautiful resort. It was wonderful; we laid low, but enjoyed the sunshine and had some good food. It was really good to get away from home, doctors and all the routine we had for the last three years. It was a great time for my husband to relax. He had been feeling pretty well at the time we went. The chemo had been over for a month or so and he was feeling a little stronger.

On Friday night before we left to come home on Saturday, he mentioned he had a bad headache. Once we were home, he went to the doctor because the headache was not letting up. X-rays were taken and it was discovered that he had some brain lesions behind his eyes. There were a few radiation treatments to eliminate the lesions. It worked, but then the cancer began to spread to his bones. This was the first time I really remember that he would complain. The pain was becoming unbearable and he was having to take some very strong pain medication. He had worked for almost three and one half years through this journey, but for the first time, he said he could not continue to work.

I knew life was about to make another serious turn for us and I was scared, I was taking Kodak moments in my head to hang on to the memories. I was doing all that I could to help make him comfortable. I wanted to honor him and respect whatever he wanted. I once said to him, I was concerned about how much pain medication he was taking, but the doctor said he could take as much and as often as he wanted. I didn't want him to become addicted. What a silly thing to be worried about when he was suffering greatly. We were a very affectionate couple so when my husband asked me not to touch him anymore because of the pain, I knew how serious it was.

Therefore we do not lose heart. Though outwardly we are wasting away, yet inwardly we are being renewed day by day. For our

*light and momentary troubles are
achieving for us an eternal glory that
far outweighs them all. So we fix
our eyes not on what is seen, but on
what is unseen, since what is seen
is temporary, but what is unseen
is eternal.*

—2 Corinthians 4:16-18

In August of that year, my aunt, who was like another mom to me, had a terrible car accident and ended up in rehab at a nursing home for two months. She had never been married and I was the one to help her and do for her. I was so overwhelmed and stressed. It was so much to care for my husband and now her. I was very thankful that my mom could come and help to feed her at times. She was not able to eat by herself. I was responsible for all of her paperwork and legal affairs. By the grace of God, my husband was able to go and sit with her sometimes since he wasn't working any more.

That was so crazy to see the sick helping the sick. My aunt loved my husband and vice versa. It was a sweet gesture and very helpful for me. I was still working through all of this. Only by

God's grace was I able to get through all of it and continue to work. After two months of rehab, my aunt was released to go home. I was thankful but was still helping to care for her.

One early Sunday morning I awoke to an empty bed. My husband had gotten up early and I found him sitting in the sunroom. When I found him, he told me that we needed to go to the emergency room. He was coughing a lot again and having difficulty breathing. We were moved into a room in the ER and the nurse starting asking questions. I was reminded that through the years of his illness, I learned that there was a time that my husband wanted to go to school to become a doctor. I guess I was not surprised. He asked so many questions when we would be at the hospital or a doctor's office, mostly because he was so interested in the knowledge and science of medicine.

This day was no different, as bad as he felt, he continued to ask many questions. It seemed that this time he may have had Pneumonia so they were going to admit him overnight. Interestingly enough, there were no rooms available so they put him in a room in ICU. They said it was temporary until there was another room ready for him. I can tell you that this was God-ordained because it ended up that is exactly where he needed to be. After they got him admitted, it was early evening. He was sitting up and chatting with everyone coming in the room. It came time for me to leave. He seemed ok, other than needing medical attention, so I went home to get some rest.

Monday morning, I was anxious to get back to the hospital to see him, but when I walked in the door, I was not prepared for what was to come next. He was lying down and not very coherent! The nurse asked me if he had a living will, I said yes and did I need to go get it. She said that I should and it might be a good time to start getting the family there.

Whoa, I thought, I knew the moment was coming, but we are never prepared. I left and once in the car, I called my youngest daughter to ask her to come. She was already headed in our direction. She has always been able to discern and is one step ahead of me in anticipation of my needs. That is truly one of her God given gifts to me and others. I am so thankful for her. She was one of the closest to us at the time logistically of all the girls, so she arrived first. I then called my husband's oldest daughter, who lived in Alabama, and knew it would be just a few hours until she could get there. She was having her mother call her two sisters, one who lived in Washington State, the other one was living in England at the time. I called my oldest daughter who was living in Mexico. There was a lot of distance for three of the girls to travel. My other stepdaughter was just thirty minutes away and my youngest had contacted her to come.

I picked up the living will and got back to the hospital as fast as I could. Once back in the room, I tried to speak to my husband and he got angry with me and told me to stop treating him so badly. This was a person that I did not know, I was taken aback.

He continued to be agitated. He would try and get out of his bed and kept saying I have got to go, which I learned later that when transitioning to end of life, one can get very agitated and want to leave this earth with their bodies. In a strange way, I found that to be fascinating, but felt sorry for him.

A pulmonary therapist would come in to try and administer forced air to him. My husband was fighting it. The therapist told me that it had the same feeling as drowning when they are forcing air into your lungs. I asked him to stop. I didn't want to see him struggle any more. It was a terrible sight to see. He had been through enough.

Some months before, I had told my husband that I was ok if and when he was ready, to stop all of his treatments. He had endured more than any one person should have to go through to try and get well. I do not like what chemo and radiation do to a body. Maybe it can help sometimes, but it is cruel and can be deadly. It depletes the body of anything good and kills our immune systems. The side effects can be nothing short of torture. That is my personal opinion. I will say that all of those that cared for my husband throughout his journey were wonderful, we were very blessed to have such a great team of nurses and staff.

That Monday night we had many come to visit my husband to include our church small group, many other friends and of course we had family there. That was another God thing. We were in ICU, so there should never be more than a couple of visitors in the room at a time, but the staff sort of turned their back to what was happening. It was wonderful to have so many loved ones and we circled his bed to pray for him. I was so blessed to have so many that cared for my husband.

Later that night, my youngest daughter and I were staying with my husband. Even though they had him sedated by this time, he still would sit up in bed at times and get agitated. Well, here is kind of a funny story, at least afterwards looking back it was funny. It was into the early morning hours and my daughter was sitting with my husband while I walked out to the lobby. The fire alarm went off and oh my goodness, I was so startled. All of the doors locked so I couldn't get back in to ICU. The sliding door to my husband's room locked and my daughter could not get out. She was the most freaked out because she was wondering if my husband tried to get out of the bed with just her in there, what was she to do? We already had enough to deal with then, but once it was all over, it gave us a little something to laugh about.

Earlier on Monday, a woman from Palliative Care came to talk to us about the situation and explained to us that he probably had just a couple of days left. We had the option of taking him home and call Hospice or putting him in another room there to keep him comfortable under Palliative care. I chose to not take him home since it was going to be so soon and I wasn't really sure how I would feel about him dying in our home. I am thankful for the choice that I made.

On Tuesday, the daughters from England and Washington State made it in. My husband was moved to another room on the third floor. The staff made it very comfortable for us, they brought more chairs in so that we could receive visitors and many came. A couple of my friends brought in food for all of us.

What an amazing blessing we had in a community that gathered together to care for us. The daughters that were there and I took shifts to sit with him through the night. Wednesday came and my husband was still with us. We were still waiting on my oldest daughter to arrive from Mexico. She finally got in very late morning if I recall. The lady from Palliative care came to speak with us. They were surprised that my husband was still hanging on. We learned that the human will is very strong when transitioning to eternity. She told us that sometimes a loved one does not want their family or specific ones around when they pass, so they will hang on until they are not there, so she suggested that we might put a 'do not disturb' sign on the door and leave for a while.

We were planning to do as she suggested. We put the sign on the door and had turned the lights off. A very close friend of mine and my husband's was there and agreed to stay behind in the corner to watch him since he still would get agitated. As we were all sitting there and getting ready to go, I looked at my husband and I saw that his breathing was changing and I felt it was time. I said to my family I think it is his time now. We all circled the bed, all of our daughters had made it, and there were two sons-in-law there along with our friend. My husband's youngest daughter suggested that we say the Lord's Prayer and we did.

I was standing at my husband's feet, I wanted his children to be able to be closer to his face. I said to him, honey, you have been the rock of our family! He had not been able to communicate with us for a couple of days, but I knew that the hearing is the last to go so that he would hear us. His oldest daughter turned to me and said that I had been the rock, I looked at my husband and he had a big smirk on his face. That was so awesome to see, what a gift for us. I then said to him that he could go home to Jesus now, immediately, he took his last breath and stepped into eternity with Jesus.

I was celebrating in my heart. I was so thankful that there was mercy and he would not ever have to suffer again. I am confident that he waited on all of our girls to get there. He adored every one of them and they meant more to him than they will ever know. Even though it was a hard time, it was a very spiritual time – and, what an honor to witness my husband taking that last breath and walking into the arms of Jesus. What a beautiful moment that must have been for him.

> *For I am already being poured out like a drink offering and the time for my departure is near. I have fought the good fight, I have finished the race, and I have kept the faith. Now there is in store for me the crown of righteousness, which the Lord, the righteous Judge, will award to me on that day—and not only to me, but*

> *also to all who have longed for his*
> *appearing.*
>
> —2 Timothy 4:6-8

Just as it is God's miracle when a baby is born, so is it a miracle when we pass from this world to the next. It was quite the journey of grace what we experienced in those four years. God loves us so much that He sent his Son to die for us and raised him from the dead so that when we leave this earth, we can have eternal life in God's Kingdom where He lives and reigns for-ever and ever.

> *Then I saw "a new heaven and a new*
> *earth," for the first heaven and the*
> *first earth had passed away, and*
> *there was no longer any sea. I saw*
> *the Holy City, the new Jerusalem,*
> *coming down out of heaven from*
> *God, prepared as a bride beauti-*
> *fully dressed for her husband. And*
> *I heard a loud voice from the throne*
> *saying, "Look! God's dwelling place*
> *is now among the people, and he*
> *will dwell with them. They will be*

his people, and God himself will be with them and be their God. 'He will wipe every tear from their eyes; there will be no more death or mourning or crying or pain, for the old order of things has passed away"

—Revelation 21: 1-4

CHAPTER TWELVE

WHO AM I?

It was a long, lonely, quiet night! How was I going to enter into the bedroom? It would be the very first time going to bed without my husband, soul mate, and best friend after his death. It was as though my body didn't want to move from the sofa. I was stuck emotionally, therefore, I couldn't will my body to move. I was tired and weary. I was scared to enter into that place where we spent our most intimate times. I knew that I was going to crumble. I was resisting. If I just stayed where I was, I wouldn't have to face it.

We had a beautiful memorial service for my husband, there were so many people that came and I was humbled by how many loved him. My son-in-law and Yoda gave a message at the service. Another son-in-law, a dear friend who my husband worked with, and one of my closest friends, gave the eulogy. It was a good day of celebrating a life that we all loved. All of our girls and families were there, along with my sister-in-law and her husband, my mom, and my aunt. There was a reception at the church and I was so thankful to all of those that prepared the food. It was wonderful.

In the next couple of days, one by one, my family members began to leave and eventually, the house was empty. Two of my very dear friends, to include my earthly angel, showed up to my surprise, to help with getting the house back in order. My earthly angel had already planned to stay the first night with me after my family left. I was so very thankful and blessed. She has always been a step ahead of me knowing what I might need. God always knows what we need and is around every corner. She helped me put off the inevitable.

In days and weeks to come there was so much to do. There was paperwork and financial affairs to take care of. There was a time of waiting on the death certificate before much could be taken care of and addressed. I was so grateful that I helped with all of our financial and household affairs – it was hard enough knowing all of that information. I could not imagine if I had not known anything about our financial affairs. If you, or someone you know, is in a marriage and has not a clue as to how to take care of any of this, I suggest you learn, and encourage them to do so, as well.

Even knowing all that I did, I hit a stumbling block. My husband stored all of our passwords for everything. I knew exactly where they were and it was very helpful, until I tried to unfreeze my credit in order to take care of a few things. The password for one of the bureaus was nowhere to be found. I was livid with him and he wasn't even there to defend himself. It was such a difficult situation to resolve. I might have fussed at him more at that time than I ever did while he was with me. I would just pray to God to please help me. Another thing that happened was when I called the only credit card company that we used to tell them that he had passed away and to please remove him from the account, I learned that I was only an authorized user, so once they learned of his death, they immediately closed the account and I was left with no credit.

Well, I am a stickler about not using or abusing credit cards, but I wanted just one. You can't imagine how long it took for me to find a company that would give me one. I had perfect credit, but as an authorized user the credit counted for him not me. I knew that because of my business that I was in, but had no idea I was just the authorized user.

Pay attention to these kind of details, it may seem small, but in the scheme of things, it was a big deal and was one more thing I had to deal with during the transition. All of what we go through when a loved one dies is very stressful, so the more you know, the better off you will be. It is so critical for me to emphasize how important it is for us to be well-educated about these things.

After my husband's death, there was a hard transition of our lives that we each had to face. When our girls and families went home, I knew it was going to be very hard for each one of them. I learned so many things about grief and one of them is that everyone in a family unit grieves differently and it is best to respect each where they are. We respond differently and move through our grief at a different pace. We should not judge the next person in how they are grieving. It is important to pay attention though and make sure that no one grieves and gets depressed to the point where they are a threat to their own life. Having faith in Jesus Christ has a huge impact on how we perceive the death of a loved one. I know that my husband was saved and would be with Our Heavenly Father throughout eternity. Because I, humbly and thankfully, have a personal relationship with Jesus Christ, I know that I will see my husband again along with my other family members.

Eternity in heaven is a promise from God and I look forward to the fulfillment of that promise. Now, even though I am saved, doesn't mean that it hasn't been hard for me. God never said that as believers we would not face trials and temptations. There have been so many milestones to walk through since his death, each one year mark, whether it was a birthday, holidays, or our anniversary; a grandchild being born, accomplishments made by any of our daughters and families, and the list goes on.

Every time something good happens and sometimes when it is not so good, I think of how much he would want to know or would enjoy celebrating or would be so excited to meet a new grandchild and just hang out with them or would want to comfort us.

We had so many plans for our future, to retire and travel, to see the world, to spend more time with our families, and so on. We used to threaten our girls that we were going to buy an RV and park in each of their driveways for two months at a time. That was a really fun dream to contemplate together. Of course, that might have been why a couple of our girls moved to where you couldn't get to them by land – just sayin'!

As I mentioned in the last chapter, my husband and I knew from the beginning of his diagnosis that God was going to use our journey for his Glory, we just didn't know how. I know that my husband made a huge impact on many as to how he walked out his cancer journey in faith and hope, always trusting Jesus Christ, whether he would live or die. Maybe I was the most inspired. He taught me so much about having such a positive attitude; that is half the battle, you know. He never complained, until close to the end, and it was certainly justified.

He never doubted God or got angry at Him, although it would have been okay if he did because God has big shoulders. It was so amazing to see how strong his faith became through those four years. He leaned on God always and stayed in the Word. He was my spiritual leader and I leaned much from him about our loving Father.

> *"But the fruit of the Spirit is love, joy, peace, forbearance, kindness, good-ness, faithfulness, [23] gentleness and self-control. Against such things there is no law. "*
>
> —Galatians 5: 22-23

Once I began to finish all that needed to be done, the numbness was wearing off and the grief was becoming more real. I was in a fog, nothing was clear, the pain was sometimes unbearable. I knew that I had to find another focus, to look at someone else's pain. I had been searching my heart and asking God what to do with all that I had gone through. I felt that I would even-tually mentor other widows. I was passionate about that. There is a season for everything, and it was a time to take care of my healing with God's help. I was still taking care of the needs of my aunt. I had my mom and friends to talk to, and that brought me comfort. My mom had lost her husband to cancer, so we had a lot to share. I was thankful for her my whole life. There is nothing like having a mother to share about your life and cry on her shoulders. She is dearly missed today.

I had gone back to work a week after my husband's service. It just seemed the best thing to do, to keep busy. It was hard to stay focused. I had a wonderful boss and friend. He took good care of me and would take over with my customers at a moment's notice, as he did for the last days of my husband's life. I will forever be grateful to you, my friend.

Going back to church was extremely hard. That is where my husband and I had met, were married and where we celebrated the end of his life. We had so many wonderful couple and single friends there and both of us were very active, both together and apart. It sort of felt like our second home. We spent a lot of time there. As time went by, being in the church among people who knew us as a couple, began to feel strange to me. As the dynamics would have it, I would feel like I was being separated from so many of our friends because we no longer had anything in common except, of course, Jesus. It is just normal, I believe, for that to happen, but I didn't like it. I felt like an outcast. I knew it was time to look elsewhere and start a new journey for just me. It was time to figure out what Deborah looked like without a husband and create a new me.

The second year as a widow was upon me and life seemed to get harder. I was having difficulty moving through the day. My heart was hurting even more. I was torn up on the inside with gut wrenching sorrow! There was a morning that I woke up and knew that if I didn't reach out for help, I might not want to wake up at all one day. As God would have it, a friend of mine had just recently told me about a Christian counselor that had helped her so much. I reached out to her that day to get his information. What a Godsend he was. I spent a year with him and came out a different person. Thank you God for always being a step ahead of me. You are my sovereign God!

> *The* Lord *is close to the broken-hearted and saves those who are crushed in spirit.*
>
> —Psalms 34:18

You see, there was so much grief that had stored up in me that there was nothing that was going to get me through it but the love and grace of Jesus Christ and those that He provided to help me. I believe the connection with my counselor was God ordained.

I was at another point of surrender in my life and he was there to help me get through the valley to become stronger in my faith and healing. Since I had lost my brother and my father, there was no one in my immediate family I could share that grief with, however my husband was there for me to lean on. Now, that he was gone, the wind had been sucked out of me. Some of the counseling was to allow me to work through the grief of each of my loved ones who had passed on by that time. I had to write letters about my grief regarding each of them. It was extremely therapeutic and helpful, but painful, at the same time. We have to be willing to walk through the pain to heal. Once I went through it, there was such a strong sense of freedom – a release of the burdens. I had to work through forgiveness for my mom even though what happened to me was not intentional on her part. It was just the way she was able to handle things.

In one of my sessions, I expressed that all of my security was gone. My dad had always rescued me and taken care of me no matter what happened. He was always there for me, then he left me in this world without him. I then leaned on my husband for my security. I knew he would always take care of me and be there for whatever happened. He was taken away from me and now what?

The counselor and I were in prayer over my security situation, and I had just expressed what I am telling you, when the counselor asked me to tell him what Jesus was telling me. I was quiet in prayer and thought for a while and then the emotions came flooding out as I said, Jesus told me that He is my security, my rock, my refuge and my strength. I was so relieved and so humbled to be reminded of what Jesus is for me and others. I was ashamed that I had put the men in my life before Him and asked for forgiveness. God is a forgiving God! I had such a sense of peace and knew that I could move forward always looking towards Jesus.

There were many victories to celebrate but one in particular stands out in my mind. Ever since my father had passed away, I really had a hard time venturing out too far by myself and then to not have my husband with me anymore, the thought of traveling alone very far frightened me and sent me into panic mode. We talked and prayed through it. The enemy likes to use our circumstances to cause fear and anxiety.

Of course, I had already come to an understanding in my heart that Jesus is my security and He really is my everything. I didn't need anyone else. I had been in a state of feeling imprisoned. My daughter and her family had recently moved to South Carolina from Mexico and I really wanted to be able to drive to visit them often. It was Christmas day and because of the counseling and all that we had worked through, I made my first drive over to her house. I was so excited about the victory that God had over me. My daughters were both elated and the daughter that I visited came out to greet and cheer me on. Of course, I am thinking that I am like a child who has made a huge accomplishment! I am God's child and He has been faithful.

That year was a huge turning point for me. I had started attending a different church with my daughter and was really enjoying it. I joined a life group of women, mostly single and was really enjoying getting to know them. I was still working through my grief but it wasn't nearly as hard as it was earlier. It is different for everyone. We never get over grief, we just move through it. Time moved on and I was creating a new me in my every day journey of His grace.

CHAPTER THIRTEEN

WHAT ARE
YOUR DREAMS

"What are your dreams," he asked me. As I sat quiet for a moment, I realized I couldn't answer that question because the one person I was to share my dreams and my future with was no longer with me. The future looked empty. I was living each day in survival mode. It was a very emotional time and I was asked to explore my heart about what it was that I wanted to do with my future.

The previous year my aunt had taken another fall and ended up in the hospital with a brain bleed. She and I had many visits to the emergency room and some overnight stays in the hospital over a several year period. It got to a point that I would kid her and say that if she really wanted to see me to just ask, that she did not have to go to the hospital to get my attention. She would laugh. She was so precious to me. I loved to make her laugh when she was not feeling well. We had an amazing relationship, one that I will never forget and will be forever thankful. She had always been so strong-headed and strong-willed. She had never married or had children. She loved and was very devoted to her career in the early days. She was the first female officer for the company she worked for. I was so proud of her accomplishments.

Since she was so strong-willed, she could be a nuisance at times (that might be an understatement), but I loved her just the same. She had moved to where I was living after my youngest was just a year old. She had retired on disability and moved closer to us so she could be of help with my children. My aunt was a God-send and such a blessing to us. I was so thankful that my girls were able to have a similar relationship with her as I did.

This last time she was admitted to the hospital was different than all of the others. I always said she was like a cat with nine lives, she would always bounce back.

This time, she became unconscious and I was told that she would probably not come out of it. After spending the day and evening in her room, while the medical staff had gotten her settled in, I went home for the evening.

The next morning I went back to check on her, expecting that there would be no response from her, just like the night before. I walked in with a cheerful tone in my voice, saying "good morning," expecting quiet. She said in her very strong voice, "Good morning". She startled me! That was just like something she would do. I was so thankful to still be able to communicate with her.

The doctor told me that she was near to end-of-life and it would be best to transition her to hospice, so we moved her into a facility where she was taken good care of with twenty-four hours of care. Typically a person who is admitted to a hospice facility only has days or a week or so before they will pass, but of course my aunt was an exception. She seemed to be an exception to every rule in life now that I think of it. She lived for three more months.

So many people came to visit her. She was dearly loved by many, especially those visitors from her church. I was thankful for all of those that would come in to visit and pray for her. The staff who cared for her spent a lot of time getting to know her and became quite fond of her. My aunt would make them laugh. They got to know her really well because she was there for so long.

One evening her nurse told me her time was near. Some of the staff that was off duty came back in that night, just to see her, and a few of them began to sing and pray. It was a sweet moment. My daughters were there with me and it was a beautiful evening. The process of dying in a Christian's life is a beautiful miracle just as a baby's birth, as we pass from this world into eternity with our Lord and Savior Jesus Christ. She left us the next morning when no one was with her. Even though those of us left behind would grieve the void and loss of my aunt, we celebrated knowing that she, who loved Jesus with her whole heart, was in the arms of our loving Father. She had said for several years she didn't know why God continued to keep her on this earth and now she had her heart's desire – to be in the presence of God.

Five months had gone by since my aunt passed away. I was busy handling all of her affairs, trying to get back on track with life and work until I received a call from my mom to come and take her to the doctor. That was very unusual for her. She worked hard at being self-reliant. She never wanted to burden me, she was not a burden but in her mind she was. My mom had lost her husband some years before so she was alone. I knew that her last few years she didn't feel up to par. She always loved being at home, she was a wonderful homemaker and the best cook ever. She had begun to slow down.

It made me sad to see that she couldn't do all the things that she most loved anymore. It is so hard to watch our elderly parents begin to decline in their health and be more dependent on others. It is so important for them to hang on to their dignity. For me it was an honor to care for both my mom and my aunt as they had certainly given most of their years caring for me. In that last year I would go and spend more time with my mom just sitting in her den talking or watching a movie with her. That made her heart smile, which all she really desired was time with me. I am sorry that I didn't do it more often and earlier, but she was so gracious that she would have never been upset by my absence or said anything about it. It was certainly one of those life lessons that time is so important with those whom we love. I am as guilty as any one, we get so busy in our lives that we forget to slow down for the people that are most important. I would say not to wait for an invitation, but to make an effort to be there.

My mom always hosted and cooked our Christmas Eve meal for many years, and let me tell you, there is no one that provided hospitality like her; she was the hospitality queen and cooked the best food you have ever had. When she made the decision that she did not feel like doing it anymore, it was a wakeup call for me and the rest of my family.

I took mother to the doctor and the words that came out of his mouth was not at all what I was expecting. She had been having a lot of problems with her back, digestive issues, not being able to eat much, and always having a sense of feeling full. She was becoming bloated all the time and very uncomfortable. The doctor felt her stomach and looked at me, saying to take her straight to the emergency room.

That was the beginning of another life changing occurrence. Once in the emergency room, she was poked and prodded, checked over, and had a lot of tests run, to find out that they wanted to release her. They said that there was nothing they could find wrong with my mom that qualified under the Medicare regulations to allow her to stay and be admitted. My mom could hardly stand up or move around on her own and she was miserable.

My step-brother (who had come to be with me), and I were furious! I didn't feel like she needed to be at home. An ambulance had to take her back to the house for me because I couldn't physically transport her. Once we were there, I realized quickly that I needed to find some help overnight because she would need more help than my back could stand. The doctor had instructed me to get her an appointment with an oncologist the next morning. It was all so interesting because no one had mentioned the 'C' word at this point.

I made the appointment and then had to have an ambulance come take her to go back to the hospital building where we had just come from the day before for the oncologist appointment. By this time my mother could not walk any more.

We saw the doctor and he admitted her right away to the hospital that sent her home less than twenty four hours prior. Within a couple of days my mom and I were told that she had cancer and it had metastasized in other parts of her body. He told us that there was nothing to be done and it would be best to send her to a hospice facility – which ended up being the same as my aunt had been in just five months before. That was a whirlwind of a few days and I was very frustrated with the entire process.

I walked into the hospice facility just minutes after the ambulance got there. I was very familiar, of course, with the facility and the staff. One of the CNA's that I recognized had just moved my mom into a room. I looked at her, she then knew who I was and remembered my mom from visiting my aunt. She asked me if that was my mom and I confirmed yes. I saw what room she put her in and panicked because it was the room where my aunt passed away just months before. She recognized what I was thinking and immediately moved my mother across the hall. May God bless her for responding to my reactions! I was so grateful for her.

I was spending most of my time with my mom. I would leave occasionally to do a little work. I was so blessed to have a few friends of mine, and hers, who would come and sit with her when I needed to leave. It is hard when you are an only child and not having siblings to depend on for help, however some of my friends would say that having siblings sometimes doesn't matter, the process is difficult no matter.

Over the years, God has given me some beautiful sisters in Christ who have stepped into that role countless times for me. They will never know how much they truly mean to me. My daughter, who lived close by, wanted to be there, but had a new baby to manage so she would come when she could; she was always there for support. My oldest daughter lived more than an hour away, but would come a few times. Two of my stepdaughters would come on occasion and my stepbrother and his wife, as well.

My mom was in hospice for five weeks. She was the most relaxed and peaceful I had seen her in a very long time. She was so very tired, she had suffered much through her life time. She would say some of the funniest things though. Her friends and I were there one day with her and she was cracking us up. Sometimes she would be so hilarious that I had to leave the room and go outside to quit laughing. It will forever be a wonderful memory for me in the midst of knowing I would soon be losing her.

One day we were having a conversation and I asked her how she was feeling; knowing that she would be dying soon. She told me she was ready, but that she was scared. I inquired of what she was scared of and she let me know that she was scared for me being left behind and alone. What she meant by being alone is that there would be no more of my immediate family. I assured her that I was going to be ok, that I had the girls and their families, along with all of my wonderful friends, but most importantly, I have our loving Father to care and provide for me.

I had so many wonderful talks with the staff as they were teaching me about the dying process. Although I was sad about what was to come, it was fascinating to me to watch how the body begins to shut down and knowing that once the dying takes their last breath, as a Christian, they will be whole again in the arms of Jesus. That is a miracle and one that I look forward to.

I was awakened to a call early one morning to say that it would be any time before my mom would pass away. I battled in my mind whether to take a shower or throw my clothes on and just go. I decided to take a shower before leaving. Once I arrived, I learned that my mom had just passed. One of the CNA's whom I adored told me she was with my mom when she died. I went in to see her and said my last good bye until I would see her again in heaven.

It was very hard losing my mom, but I was relieved that she was not in pain or suffering anymore. It really isn't about us when our loved ones are hurting so much. We want to make it about us because we are sad, but it is so important that we pay attention to the needs and desires of our loved ones. I had told my mom several times that it was ok for her to leave this earth. I am told that we have such a strong will that the person dying can will their selves to hang on for a little while or to let go.

I struggled with not being there to hold her hand as she was passing from this world into God's kingdom. Had I not taken that shower, maybe I would have made it in time. I had to resolve that by believing two things, that possibly my mom didn't want me there at that time. She was always very protective of me, so that would make sense, and, helped me make peace with it. I also know that our God is sovereign and my ways are not His ways. I had to let that thinking go because it could make me a little crazy. I wanted to focus on the times that I was with her and know that I did everything I could to take care of her the best way I knew how. God is so gracious with us and I needed to be the same with myself.

Early the following year, I had hired a production coach. I was a mortgage loan officer and had been for 24 years. Because of all the losses and caregiving I had undertaken for about eight years, my business production had suffered. The previous year, I had taken care of all of my mom and aunt's affairs and was ready to make a new start with my life. I had decided it was time to take care of me personally, spiritually, physically, and business-wise, which resulted in hiring the production coach. I had met him on another occasion and knew that he was a Christian, which was a big reason for hiring him, particularly.

In our first conversation, he started asking me about my dreams and that is when I became very emotional realizing that all my dreams had been wrapped up in my husband. He got me thinking about what I wanted to do with the rest of my life. He encouraged me to create a dream board, which I still have a picture of today. As I began to put the dream board together, putting Christ in the center of that board, everything started to unfold. I could see that I was to serve God in a ministry, although I didn't know what area just yet.

For years, I had mentioned that I wanted to write a book, so that went on my board. I wanted more time with family, especially my grandchildren. Today I have had three 'Meema camps' for them and it has been a blast. I am so blessed! I wanted to travel more. I get to do that with my Wellness business now and love it. I wanted to do more about my health, and I have. I wanted more time with friends and have had the pleasure of not only having time with them, but God has connected me with so many more beautiful women and new friendships over the years.

There had only been a few coaching sessions when I began to realize that God wanted me to walk away from the business I was in to serve Him. God used my coach as a vessel and coached me right out of my mortgage career. As far as I was concerned, I was to be in the business for at least five more years. God prompted me with other plans.

I was sixty at the time and knew I needed to be there until I could receive Medicare benefits and certainly still needed income, as I was providing for myself after losing my husband. Well, God had other plans. He knew that I was at such a vulnerable place in my life, that it would be when I would be ready and willing to say Yes to His call. I did say YES and had the faith that He would show me what He wanted me to do and that He would provide all that I needed if I took that big LEAP of FAITH.

I was at another point of surrender in my life. I went to my boss to say that I was resigning. He was like a son to me and I adored him. He told me that he wasn't surprised as to why I was leaving and gave me his blessings. My last day of work was in December. I didn't really know where God was taking me or how He was going to use me, but I was excited to embark on an incredible journey of grace.

"For my thoughts are not your thoughts, neither are your ways my ways," declares the LORD. "As the heavens are higher than the earth, so are my ways higher than your ways and my thoughts than your thoughts"
—Isaiah 55:8-9

CHAPTER FOURTEEN

FAITH WALK

There I was, standing by the room on the third floor where my husband died. My breath was taken away! It was the first time I had been there since he had been gone. I had signed up to take a Pastoral Care Education class in our local hospital at the beginning of January, after leaving my previous job. I was taken on a tour of the entire building and found myself in several places where several of my loved ones had been.

After having experienced three deaths of family members and being in the hospice environment, I realized that I had a heart and passion for the families of the dying and the one that was transitioning from this world to the next. I had mentioned before that I found the dying process to be fascinating and such a miracle that only God could design. When I said yes to God's call, I was feeling as though I was to become a Hospice Chaplain. That was my reason for starting the Pastoral Care class.

In December, the month that I was resigning, I had run into a longtime friend and she looked frazzled. I had not seen her in years. Upon inquiring of her as to how she was doing, I learned that she was juggling a lot of responsibilities in her life. Her mother had recently been admitted to rehab because of a fall. My friend was also responsible for another family member with disabilities and was feeling so torn as to how to care for both, and overwhelmed. It was a God-ordained appointment.

Since I was learning about how I loved sitting with those that are sick, I offered to help her. That was the beginning of another way that God was showing me my heart. I would go and spend time with her mom every week. She would light up when I walked into the room, not because of who I am but because of who Jesus was through me. She loved Jesus and loved to hear me read scripture. We had many awesome conversations about Jesus, her family, and life.

I became her confidant and she would share with me about end of life thoughts that she might not have shared with those who were close to her. I was truly humbled to know her. Once she was out of rehab and back home, I would continue to visit. There was a time that my friend had to take her mom to the emergency room, she called me right away and asked if I would come and be with them.

Another time, there was to be some surgery and she asked me to be by their side. I was definitely learning more about ministering to others from class and from my experiences. As my friend's mom neared end of life, I was visiting more often and had the honor to sit with her on the same day of her death, just hours before she passed away. What an honor and a privilege to know someone that intimately. I remember sitting at her funeral and, as it ended, hearing God say," Your job is finished here."

That was such a bittersweet moment, but rewarding to know that I had been obedient to His call.

God has continued to put other women in my life to do the same, to journey with them as they transition to the end of life. It has been a beautiful experience with many. When one would pass away, God would show me someone else to journey with. What an amazing God we serve. I was on a journey to learn more about my heart and for healing.

God gave me the opportunity to journey with a family friend who was a really close friend of my mom's. In the earlier days, she and her husband were very good friends with both of my parents. When my parents divorced, many of their friends stopped having anything to do with my dad, and he was so hurt! I understood that he had hurt my mom, and there was no excuse for that, and I was truly sorry for her pain, but I didn't understand the rejection from his friends.

I would hear of his closest friends and golf buddies being ugly to him and saying very unkind words. Regardless of what my dad had done, I had always loved him. He was my daddy, so if he was hurt, then I was hurt and I was angry.

When my dad passed away, only one of their friends acknowledged to me that she cared about him and his death. I have always had an easy time forgiving others but this time, I hung on to that bitterness in my heart for years with so many of their friends. They were all like family to me and it all changed. There came a time that I knew I needed to forgive them and I would ask God every time I would see one of them, how many more times would I have to forgive? It was so hard and really it was my pride that was in the way.

> *"Then Peter came to Jesus and asked,*
> *"Lord, how many times shall I forgive*
> *my brother when he sins against me?*
> *Up to seven times? Jesus answered,*
> *"I tell you, not seven times but seven-*
> *ty-seven times."*
> —Matthew 18:21-22

When I heard that my mom's friend was sick, I knew I was to reach out to her, and, let me tell you; that was not easy. I had to swallow a lot of pride. I ended up journeying with her throughout her days until death. I had forgotten how much I adored her and her family. I was so excited to be able to reconnect with all of her children. When we were all young adults we had a blast hanging out together. They all lived a distance away so it wasn't always easy for them to get to their mom. I could get to her quickly when they were concerned. I spent at least one time a week with her and was so honored to hear so many of her stories about her and her husband and family and discuss memories of long ago of my parents and all of their friends.

I became her confidant as well as she shared many intimate thoughts about her last days. I never said anything to her about my feelings all of those years because I discerned that she was probably oblivious to how she and others had made me feel. I felt that the time spent with her was about her and not about me. I was there to hear her heart. Quietly from my heart, I did forgive her, and all of the others. By letting go of the bitterness, I felt a freeing of my spirit.

God was ordaining every connection and sending me on an emotional journey of healing. When I said yes and surrendered to Him, I had no idea where He was taking me on my faith walk. Once, after I had started my class, another friend of mine connected me with someone she knew who was a Chaplain, to have a conversation with him just to talk to and learn from. When I sat with him and told him of my plans to be a Chaplain, he said something I found to be very profound. He suggested that I always keep my heart open because God may have other plans for me. Looking back, I realize that he was exactly right but I could not see it at the time. All I could think of was being a Chaplain.

During the six months of the class I was taking, I discovered that it was as much for me personally as it was about ministering to others. God revealed much about myself and it was quite emotional. That hospital was where my husband passed away and my mom and aunt transitioned from to hospice. Sometimes I felt like that hospital was my second home. Between all three of them, I spent many days there for several years.

Here is what I find to be a comical story because if you don't laugh you would sit down and cry. My youngest daughter went into labor early one evening so off we went to the same hospital. She was in labor all night, so I was up with her without any sleep.

About six o'clock in the morning, I received a call from the assisted living facility where my aunt lived, to say they were sending her to the emergency room.

Of course they are! I told them to send her on, that I was already there and would find her once she was admitted. My daughter had her baby around eleven that morning. It was such an exciting time for both of us. My daughter was exhausted and so was I.

My mother had an appointment with a doctor at the hospital around noon or so. She could not walk far so I went down to meet her and park her car. I went to the doctor appointment with her, then put her in a wheelchair to take her to see my daughter and the baby, then off to see my aunt, after she was admitted into her room. I then took my mom back to her car, checked on my aunt to make sure she was well taken care of, checked on my daughter one more time, then I left, went home, and got straight to bed. Thank God they all were at the same hospital or I could never have done it all. It was a lot on me that day but I had to look at the positive. I was so grateful that my daughter and her baby were healthy and my two ladies were settled in. There is a silver lining in everything, if we look for it!

One evening I was serving as a Chaplain in the hospital, working through the required hours of clinicals. I found myself in the same room standing by a bed in the same space where my husband had died, as I was ministering to an elderly gentleman. It took courage to walk into that room and as I stood there, for a moment, I had a flash back with the vision of my husband lying there, then I put my focus back on the patient. I never had another issue with being in that part of the hospital again.

As I made my rounds throughout the hospital, in and out of the rooms or emergency room, I would have memories of my mom and aunt. It got easier over time and healing came. I will forever be grateful to my God for sending me on that journey. He knew that I needed more healing so that I would be able to serve others. He always has our best interest at heart and knows what we need. We have to trust Him when He leads, even though we might not have an understanding as to why or where He takes us, but trust and obey and know that He is a loving God!

"for we walk by faith, not by sight"
—2 Corinthians 5:7

Making ourselves available to the Lord, without resisting, opens us up for an adventure and experiences that are beyond anything we could ever imagine. God has been faithful in my journey of grace as He was showing me my heart and passions and had been preparing me for the plans and purpose He had yet revealed, in the days to come.

CHAPTER FIFTEEN

BIRTHING A MINISTRY

One morning as I sat quietly in prayer, God spoke to me –and, very loudly, I must add, that the name of my ministry was to be called *The Women at The WELL!* I was taken aback and so very humbled and broken, with a river of tears flowing. It felt as though He was screaming those words to me. I was beginning to have an understanding as to what God had been preparing me for throughout the previous years.

Prior to that day, over a long period of time, it seemed that everywhere I turned, God was sending me a message through something I was either reading or listening to about the story of the woman at the well, from the scriptures in the fourth chapter of John. I was paying attention, but had no idea what the significance was until that morning, when I finally, began to get it.

Years ago, God would continually give me glimpses of something I was supposed to do with a community ministry to care for others, but that is all He would show me. Now I understand that it wasn't the right time for me to know; it is in His perfect timing and will that things fall in to place and open up. God still had much to show and teach me about myself, to include healing. I just love how our sovereign God knows about our life and what He has in store for us. He is our creator and knows us before we are born. I have quoted this verse before, but it is my favorite, and, my life verse. This scripture has had a huge impact on my life.

> *"For I know the plans I have for you, declares the Lord, plans to prosper you and not to harm you, plans to give you hope and a future."*
> —Jeremiah 29:11

I have had faith in God for years, but it was not until two thousand fourteen when HE called on me and I surrendered with a big YES. It was then that He began to reveal the purpose and plans He has for me. It has been a crazy, exciting, and humbling journey, from the time I started my faith walk. It has been so surreal, like I am living in a dream. I would ask why God would you choose me. I am an ordinary woman with a big heart who loves Jesus! I have no college education and have never attended seminary. I am not a bible scholar, but do know how to love and care for those who are hurting. I am a sinner and have made poor choices that took me down the wrong paths in my life. I know the love of Jesus and His grace. I have learned from my life experiences about my heart and the heart of others. God called ordinary people to be His disciples from all walks of life. He uses us where we are and allows us to go through life's struggles and hardships so that we can be molded into how He wants to use us for the good of others. I am humbled and honored to be able to serve our Heavenly Father. I cannot serve in this ministry without God. His grace is sufficient and He equips me with all that I need. I am nothing without Him.

"But he said to me, "My grace is sufficient for you, for my power is made perfect in weakness." Therefore I will boast all the more gladly about my weaknesses, so that Christ's power may rest on me. That is why, for Christ's sake, I delight in weaknesses, in insults, in hardships, in persecutions, in difficulties. For when I am weak, then I am strong."

—2 Corinthians 12:8-10

It was amazing to see how God moved through the entire experience of preparing to launch this ministry. Before I even asked, He told me about four women to contact. I knew two of them and knew of the other two. I wasn't sure what He wanted with them, but I was obedient and set a meeting with each of them, individually. I shared with each, the vision God had given me. Two of them agreed to serve in the ministry and I was in awe at God's hand in all of this. I also asked my earthly angel to come along on this journey with me. She is my right hand woman, so to speak, as we continue to do life together.

God tapped me on the shoulders about another one of our team, whom I did not yet know. She is from the church that I attend. These ladies bring so much to our ministry and I am forever thankful for how they have trusted God and me to serve along with me. God has also connected me with some other amazing women who volunteer their time and talents to help along this journey.

Before launching, I had found a place for us to hold our events that I was really excited about. The owner of the facility had agreed and we were set, at least I thought we were, until I received a call one day from him three weeks before our first night. He told me that because of some personal reasons, he could no longer keep his commitment. That was certainly a surprise and not expected, so I said, "Ok, God, what now?"

The next day, I received a call from a friend who knew of a place that might work. I went that day to check it out and it has turned out to be a perfect location. We continue to meet there. God already knew where we would end up. He used my friend as the messenger. Our location has been perfect. I am so grateful to the owner for his graciousness and allowing us to meet there. God is sovereign, He knows our needs, and we just have to trust Him. He reveals what He wants me to know about the ministry, a little at a time. I have learned to pray, trust and listen to Him. I know He is already in tomorrow and is always preparing what He will reveal to me so I know it is best to wait on Him. I pray and embrace where we are and try not to get ahead of Him. Be still in the wait is what I have learned.

God has shown me that the ministry is to connect women with others through sharing personal stories of transformation from life struggles, pain and suffering. Our mission is to encourage, inspire and empower women to attain the living water of Hope through the love and grace of Jesus Christ. God began to show me how to have a more abundant life through hope in Him years ago and I want to share this with other women. One thing that I have learned about myself throughout my life journey is that I have a strong sense of empathy for others who are broken and have hurting hearts. It is a blessing and a curse. Sometimes, it can be such a strong feeling of sadness that it becomes over-whelming. The awesome news is that by God's grace I can lift up the burdens to Him. I do not have to carry them and neither do you.

*"For my yoke is easy and my burden
is light."*

—Matthew 11:30

Through several ministries, God has given me training to know how to use this gift, and, to help and encourage others. My passion is to walk alongside women experiencing pain and suffering – whether it be in a group or individual setting.

I prayed for a space to host the ministry, God provided that space. He has provided women to help serve in many ways to include being on my ministry team, to help greet, to give donations, and women who are gifted in music. I am always blessed to have speakers on the calendar for a year in advance. God knows our needs and He is providing them every day. I am so humbly thankful for all of the women who attend every month. I am blessed with every beautiful face that walks in that door.

You might ask, what is the significance of the woman at the well and the living water? Jesus went and sat down at the well one day because he was tired. He knew that the woman would come. The woman came and began to have conversations with Jesus. He asked her for water and she responded by saying he didn't have anything to draw the water with. Jesus said that if she knew the gift of God and who she was talking with she would have asked Him and He would have given her the living water. She said that the well was deep and He had nothing to draw it with so where would He get this living water.

> *"But whoever drinks the water I give them will never thirst. Indeed, the water I give them will become in them a spring of water welling up to eternal life."*
>
> —John 4:14

He could give her living water so she would not continue to be thirsty. She responded that she wanted the living water. He asked her to go and get her husband. She said that she did not have a husband. He told her that she was correct, that she in fact had five husbands in the past and the man she currently lived with was not her husband. Since He already knew everything about her, she recognized that maybe He was a prophet, but Jesus told her that He was the Christ.

It is such a beautiful thing that Jesus did. He did not condemn her, but was gracious to her. When she heard the news, her eyes were opened and she acknowledged Him for who He was. The woman dropped her jar at the well to go back to share with the others, saying could this be the Christ? She had left all of her life baggage, strongholds, sins and struggles with Him as she left the jar behind with Jesus. The living water is the anointing of the Holy Spirit upon receiving Jesus Christ into our hearts. Jesus came to this earth and died for us and was resurrected so that we might have eternal life with Him. All we have to do is to repent and ask Jesus into our hearts to receive salvation.

> *"For it is by grace you have been saved, through faith—and this is not from yourselves, it is the gift of God— not by works, so that no one can boast."*
>
> —Ephesians 2:8-9

There are so many unhealthy things and people that we use to try and fill up the empty spaces in our hearts and soul such as alcohol, drugs, sex, food, relationships and the list goes on. There are other things that keep us from accepting that God could love us just as we are like shame, guilt, divorce, extramarital affairs, lying, abuse, etc. These are examples of the water that the woman was drawing on to satisfy her life. Jesus was offering the living water, which is the anointing of the Holy Spirit. Once saved, He is the only one that fills up our hearts to give us joy and fulfillment.

> *"When Jesus spoke again to the people, he said, 'I am the light of the world. Whoever follows me will never walk in darkness, but will have the light of life.'"*
>
> —John 8:12

The journey of grace continues as my heart is overflowing with the love that God has for me. I am a daughter of a King that loves me so much that He carried all my sins to the cross and died for me. There is nothing that can separate me from Him as I continue to seek Him more.

"For God so loved the world that he gave his one and only Son, that whoever believes in him shall not perish but have eternal life."

—John 3:16

CHAPTER SIXTEEN

MY CUP RUNNETH OVER

"How great thou art" the song says and, yes, He is!

> *"Amazing grace how sweet the sound*
> *that saved a wretch like me. I once*
> *was lost but now am found, was*
> *blind but now I see."*

Jesus saved me from myself so many years ago and I am so humbly grateful! I have walked through many struggles and have suffered much, but He has always been right there for me to lean on. Sometimes, I didn't recognize it, but as I have grown and been allowed to walk through the valleys, I have seen how He has been trans-forming me to His greater purpose on this earth.

As a Christian, we are never promised that life will be easy, but we do have the promise from our Lord and Savior that He will never leave us or forsake us. He gives us what we need to get through the suffering. He has a purpose for each one of us. You see, it is about the entire journey on this earth.

We are just passing through and the journey is short. We are really here for just one reason and that is to walk with Jesus, to seek His face, to know Him more, to serve Him and to share the love and grace of Jesus Christ with others. We each have different gifts and talents that our God has created in us and we are to use them for His glory. It is never too late! We cannot find our purpose and passions without the struggles we face because that is how we learn. He is pruning us and removing the dead stuff so that we can blossom. He wants to give us so much in abun-dance but we have to let go of those things that hold us back, that is a stronghold in our life, the toxic relationships in our lives and the idols that we hold on to, to fill our souls. Only Jesus Christ can complete us and make us whole. Glory to

God for sending His Son to die for us and rise again to give us life in eternity.

The beautiful thing is that we can start over each morning. It doesn't matter where we have been in the past, God has already forgiven us if we have invited Him into or hearts. We just have to repent (feel or express sincere regret or remorse about one's wrongdoing or sin), and ask for forgiveness, after inviting Him to be our Lord and Savior. He gives us grace every morning, great is His faithfulness! We are all sinners in need of a Savior – Jesus Christ!

Today, I can sincerely say that I am thankful for everything that I have walked through. That doesn't mean that I am happy about the suffering or the losses I have encountered. I would love to have my husband, brother, dad, mother and aunt back on this earth. I would certainly rather not have gone through the abusive relationships that my girls and I have experienced. I would rather not have had my children live in a broken home and be separated from their father. I cannot change all that has happened, but I can choose joy that only comes from Jesus Christ.

I can choose what I do with all of the scars and pain. I choose God and to be in eternity with

Him. I choose to listen and be obedient to His call. There are many women who are broken and need Jesus and because of my pain, I can walk with them, love, understand and empathize with them and help to guide and encourage them. Had I not been through it all, I would not humbly have the honor to do what God has called me to do. I would have never paid attention to His call. I pray that I will glorify God in everything I do and give Him the glory for all good things in my life. I am not, nor will I ever be perfect in this. I fall short every day as He continues to stretch and grow me spiritually. He is strong where I am weak.

> *"You turned my wailing into dancing; you removed my sackcloth and clothed me with joy."*
> —Psalms 30:11

You might ask why is being in eternity with God such a big deal and why would we want to be saved? God has so much more in store for us in His Kingdom. I am so excited to share with you.

"Then I saw a new heaven and a new earth, for the first heaven and the first earth had passed away, and there was no longer any sea. I saw the Holy City, the new Jerusalem, coming down out of heaven from God, prepared as a bride beautifully dressed for her husband. And I heard a loud voice from the throne saying, "Now the dwelling of God is with men, and He will live with them. They will be his people, and God himself will be with them and be their God. He will wipe every tear from their eyes. There will be no more death or mourning or crying or pain, for the old order of things has passed away."

—Revelation 21:1-4

Heaven is the ultimate gift for us to look forward to! I am ready for Jesus to come back and take us home. I will get to see many of my loved ones that have passed before me. The thought of seeing them, really excites me, but what I look forward to the most is to kneel before our loving God, and be in the presence of the Holy of Holy's. You don't want to miss this opportunity. Jesus has made it so easy to be with Him. He is knocking at our hearts, but He is a gentleman and will not enter, until you open the door for Him.

Our bodies are only for this lifetime, but our spiritual bodies are for eternity. It is up to us as to what we choose for the life after.

> *"Therefore, we do not lose heart. Though outwardly we are wasting away, yet inwardly we are being renewed day by day. For our light and momentary troubles are achieving for us an eternal glory that far outweighs them all. So we fix our eyes not on what is seen, but on what is unseen. For what is seen is temporary but what is unseen is eternal."*
>
> —2 Corinthians 4:16-18

My cup is running over with an abundance of joy! God has filled up my heart in a way that I could never have imagined just because I said yes to His call and I continue to seek His will for me.

I do not boast about what I have done but boast for what the Lord has done through me. The joy is instilled in my heart forever, even though I might have days where I am lonely, discouraged, grieving with sadness, anger, or experience a broken heart. I look up to my God, to stay in prayer, to ask who I can serve, and to keep a grateful heart. I ask God to help me in my time of need and to equip me in all things He calls me to do. I ask that it be not my will, but His. The joy is always deep in my heart because of my relationship with Jesus.

I pray that God's story, through my life, might encourage or empower you. I pray that you will find the courage to dream and take action. I pray that something in these stories have resonated with you and that you will take a step of faith. It is one step at a time as God reveals what He has planned for your life. I pray that you will find hope, comfort, and strength through these pages of words that the Holy Spirit has laid on my heart. I pray that you will hear Him say to you, "I Got This" and you will walk in the truth (that will set you free), with Jesus and know He is holding you in the palm of His hands. I pray that you will find joy in your heart as you take a faith walk with Jesus on a journey of grace.

And, unlike me, I hope you will realize much earlier in life that it's okay to surrender and let go, and trust the One who can handle it all. My prayer is that you would know, at a much younger age, what I did not, what took me decades of pain and tears to learn – that He has it all. And, it's okay to trust Him with it all.

Can't you just hear Him say,

"I Got this!
–God."

"Now to Him who is able to do immeasurably more than all we ask or imagine, according to his power that is at work within us, to Him be glory in the church and in Christ Jesus throughout all generations, forever and ever! Amen."
—Ephesians 3:20

AUTHOR
DEBORAH BENNETT

Deborah Bennett (aka Debbie Bennett Gronner) is the founder and director of *The Women at The WELL*, a ministry that supports and ministers to women who have experienced brokenness and loss in life. Through a lifetime of personal struggle and pain, she has found her passion to minister to others with monthly meetings, annual retreats, and inspirational messaging.

After a 24-year career as a Mortgage Loan Officer, Bennett stepped out on faith to launch her ministry to encourage, inspire, and empower women of all walks of life.

Bennett ministers to others as God has been writing His story through her life and uses that to inspire others to healing, and grow her ministry of *The Women at the WELL.*

She is a mom and grandmother, and also enjoys health and wellness topics that support healing from the inside out. She has been inspiring men and women to take charge of their health and wellness as an independent Wellness Consultant.

ABOUT *The Women at The WELL*

*T*he *Women at The WELL* was launched in November, 2016. We are connecting women through stories of transformation from life struggles, pain and suffering. Our mission is to encourage, inspire and empower women to attain the Living Water of Hope through the love and grace of Jesus Christ.

We meet the first Thursday night of every month. We have added an evening of prayer and are praying about other ministries that I believe God is laying on my heart to be a part of a larger vision that has been given me. I am waiting on God to show me what is next. He has been connecting me with so many beautiful women with skills and gifts to bring to our ministry to be able to help women from all walks of life. There is a huge need of support for the women in the community and I am excited to see where God is going to take us next. He will direct our paths. Our God is faithful.

It has been humbling and an honor to walk this journey with those that serve beside me. I am thankful for their willing hearts. God is blessing the women who attend our events and I am beyond blessed by every one of them.